Christian Leaders
for Creation

We cannot be all that God wants us to be without caring about the earth.

>—Rev. Dr. Rick Warren, author of *The Purpose Driven Life*

The growing possibility of our destroying ourselves and the world with our own neglect and excess is tragic and very real.

>—Billy Graham

As Christians, our faith in Jesus Christ compels us to love our neighbors and to be stewards of God's creation. The good news is that with God's help, we can stop global warming, for our kids, our world, and for the Lord.

>—Rev. Joel Hunter, senior pastor of Northland,
>A Church Distributed, Longwood, Florida

When concern for economic and technological progress is not accompanied by concern for the balance of the ecosystem, our earth is inevitably exposed to serious environmental damage, with consequent harm to human beings. Blatant disrespect for the environment will continue as long as the earth and its potential are seen merely as objects for immediate use and consumption, to be manipulated by an unbridled desire for profit.

>—Pope John Paul II

If I am going to be in the right relationship with God, I should treat the things he has made in the same way he treats them.

>—Francis Schaeffer, founder of L'Abri and author
>of *How Should We Then Live?*

Did God make the world? Does he sustain it? Has he committed its resources to our care? His personal concern for his own creation should be sufficient to inspire us to be equally concerned.

—John R. W. Stott, founder of the Langham Partnership International and John Stott Worldwide Ministries

God calls me in Scripture to be a good steward of the earth.

—Steve Hayner, professor at Columbia Theological Seminary

However we treat the world, that's how we are treating Jesus because he is the cosmic glue.

—Paul de Vries, president of New York Divinity School

The present ecological crisis has occurred in large part because modern culture believes it can thrive apart from the presence of this tree of life.... Let us live in the promise of the tree of life, discovering its branches and fruit covering the earth, offering the healing and wholeness intended by our Creator.

—Wesley Granberg-Michaelson, general secretary emeritus, Reformed Church in America

Care for the earth is not just an Earth Day slogan, it is a requirement of our faith. We are called to protect people and the planet, living our faith in relationship with all of God's creation.

—"Sharing Catholic Social Teaching Reflections of the U.S. Catholic Bishops, 1998"

This is one of the few books I know of that gets *more* timely as time goes by.

—Robert R. Hudson, editor and author of *The Christian Writer's Manual of Style*

SERVING GOD

A Call to Care for Creation and Your Soul

SAVING THE PLANET

UPDATED AND EXPANDED EDITION

Previously published as *Serve God, Save the Planet*

J. Matthew Sleeth, MD

FOREWORD BY JOEL HUNTER

ZONDERVAN®

ZONDERVAN.com/
AUTHORTRACKER
follow your favorite authors

ZONDERVAN

Serving God, Saving the Planet
Copyright © 2006, 2007, 2012 by J. Matthew Sleeth, MD

Previously published as *Serve God, Save the Planet*
Hardcover edition published in 2006 by:
Chelsea Green Publishing, PO Box 428, White River Junction, VT 05001

This title is also available as a Zondervan ebook. Visit www.zondervan.com/ebooks.

This title is also available in a Zondervan audioedition. Visit www.zondervan.fm.

Requests for information should be addressed to:

Zondervan, *Grand Rapids, Michigan 49530*

Library of Congress Cataloging-in-Publication Data

Sleeth, J. Matthew, 1956–
    Serving God, saving the planet : a Christian call to action / Matthew Sleeth ;
foreword by Joel C. Hunter.
      p. cm.
    Rev. ed. of: Serve God, save the planet.
    ISBN 978-0-310-32004-3 (softcover)
    1. Human ecology—Religious aspects—Christianity. 2. Environmental ethics.
I. Sleeth, J. Matthew, 1956– Serve God, save the planet. II. Title.
BT695.5.S54 2012
261.8'8—dc23

2012043886

Dr. Sleeth's medical stories are based on his experiences in Central America and in twenty-two hospitals throughout the United States. Names, genders, ages, and some aspects of medical histories have been changed to assure the privacy of patients.

Cover design: Ron Huizinga
Cover photography: Noel Hendrickson / Getty Images
Interior design: Beth Shagene

Printed in the United States of America

---

13 14 15 16 17 18 19 /DCI/ 22 21 20 19 18 17 16 15 14 13 12 11 10 9 8 7 6 5 4 3 2 1

Thank you, first to God,
who has been loving and faithful,
and to my beautiful and supportive wife, Nancy.
I love you, and I couldn't have done this without you.

Contents

Workbook

Appendices

Foreword

You hold in your hands a survival manual, not only for our planet, but also for your spiritual life.

Oh, it's cleverly disguised with delightful and winsome personal stories, and it has all the information necessary to equip you intellectually to address a crucial cultural crisis. But don't be fooled: it is a survival manual written by a most intriguing national leader in the field.

Having heard many teachers on the subject of caring for God's creation, I was prone to be sympathetic to this book. Yet I thought I would be hammered over the head by the usual approach: "I care about this, our planet is dying, so get off your duff and do something!" But this book goes straight to the heart. It will engage you from the depths of your conscience to the heights of your aspirations for a life well lived.

What impresses me most about this book is the quality of leadership Matthew Sleeth offers. To be a persuasive leader of any cause, one must fulfill several basic requirements.

The first order of effective leadership is not information, but example. Matthew Sleeth and his family live what they recommend. Their example may seem extreme to some, but the spiritual and practical benefits of their lifestyle cannot be dismissed. Their lifestyle manifests what is really important in life.

The second order of effective leadership is competent knowledge of both the subject and audience. This book does not contain a numbing recitation of facts; we can get those from scientific studies. What it does contain is the information and logic we all need to be "equipped for every good work."

The third order of effective leadership is tireless effort, an almost intrusive kind of prophetic "I must go to other towns also" spread of the message. I do not believe there is another leader in America who has spoken in more churches than the good doctor Sleeth, and it gives me hope for the future of the church. In addition, Matthew Sleeth is making a lot of people uncomfortable. That's good because we need to be challenged, or we will not change.

The fourth order of leadership is addressing objections that will inevitably arise. There is a law in physics that mirrors the emotional/cultural/spiritual laws God created: for every action, there is an equal and opposite reaction. While this book gives intelligent response to voices that would resist a better stewardship of life and the planet, it also calls us to a more deeply moral response. There is no effective argument against doing the right thing for the right reasons.

The unique feature of this book is that it teaches us that taking care of the planet is not mainly about counting your air conditioner's BTUs or keeping your tires inflated to the right level. Taking care of the planet is about taking care of each other. In story after story, I fell in love with the characters (real people I hope to meet in heaven), and I want to be a better steward of the earth's resources for their sakes.

Most important: this book focuses us on God. Ultimately our life is not summed up in what we have or what we don't have; it is summed up in how well we have loved. And how well we have loved involves taking care of the planet God gave us. Cultivating the grape and wheat is as holy as serving them in communion. Not polluting the earth is as worshipful as building a church on it. Learning how to live simply in nature is as reverent as preaching in any gilded cathedral ever built. And loving your family is a sure way to appreciate the rest of God's family.

Serving God, Saving the Planet is full of stories that turn our hearts toward God. It turns out that Matthew Sleeth, like the gospel writer Luke before him, is not only a physician, but a prophet.

And his book is both a survival manual and prayer book.

> —Dr. Joel C. Hunter, senior pastor
> Northland—A Church Distributed
> Longwood, Florida

Introduction

Since this book launched six years ago, much has changed in my life and in the world. In the Gulf of Mexico, BP beat Exxon's long-standing record for the amount of oil spilled off America's shores. On the coast of Japan, nuclear reactors melted down after being damaged by a tidal wave. High in the Rocky Mountains, the Park Service is now advising us that Glacier National Park will soon run out of glaciers.

During these six years, my home life has also changed. Our children are no longer in high school: my son married and graduated from medical school, my daughter graduated from college. We are still a close family living within several blocks of each other, but now we all reside in the buckle of the Bible belt—Lexington, Kentucky.

Although some of the statistics and circumstances have changed since this book was penned, the principles remain the same. How can we better serve God and be a witness of his love? How can we fulfill our role as stewards and help protect this blue globe of life?

Serving God, Saving the Planet continues to open doors, acting as an "OmniPass" for me to speak from the pulpits of nearly every denomination. It has given me the privilege of talking about the environment on Christian radio and about Jesus on public radio. It has placed me in front of the camera on television shows, documentaries, and more than a dozen church curricula films. And it has repeatedly led me back to the classroom—from grade schools to college chapels to seminary convocations. I especially love to hold question and answer sessions. On several occasions, I have had to end when my voice simply gave out. It is during these times that I acutely feel the presence of the Holy Spirit.

One afternoon, a twelve-year-old attending a conference with her father asked an unsettling question—the question that most of us are too afraid to ask: "Is it too late?" Something about the young woman's face, or the sincerity in her voice, or the trust and concern in her eyes told me to consider the question carefully. *Is it too late?*

Even a cursory glance at environmental projections leads to a disheartening response. Trajectories that graph species extinction, fresh water depletion, topsoil loss, and ocean health all disappear in steep slopes off the charts. The situation does not look good. No one, regardless of their politics or religion, believes that society can continue business-as-usual for the next hundred years and have everything turn out all right. Society is simply too big and too powerful to wander into the future guided only by the self-interests of the current generation. *Is it too late?*

My answer to the twelve-year-old: I live in faith, but I work in the world. God did not stop Hitler; instead, he sent Winston Churchill and a reluctant free world to end the Holocaust. We should not expect God to miraculously prevent the glaciers from disappearing; rather, if we want to avert widespread flooding and droughts, you and I and millions of others must end the destruction of the world's largest freshwater reservoirs.

Quitting my career as a physician, writing this book, speaking in more than a thousand venues in six years—these are some of the things I have done to be able to look that young woman in the eye and tell her that yes, there is hope. With God, all things are possible.

When *Serving God, Saving the Planet* first hit the shelves, believing in both the Bible and the environment was news. But a change has occurred since its publication. The church is waking up to our biblical responsibility to care for God's earth. The tide is changing.

One of the questions I hear again and again is, "Can one person really make a difference?" It is a good question. People don't like to work in isolation or feel as though their efforts are pointless.

My first response: you are not alone. The number of people who believe in the Creator *and* in caring for his creation is constantly growing. This is because we have opened our Bibles to see what Scripture actually says about creation care. From Genesis to Revelation, it is clear that the earth belongs to the Lord, that he loves his creation, and that he holds us responsible for being good stewards.

My second answer to the *why care* question: because doing so is good work. When we feed the poor, our hearts grow full. We have a similar "well done" response when we do any of the Lord's work. There will never be an end to five-year-olds who need to be taught how to read. Kindergarten teachers do not wipe out illiteracy; rather, they do the good work of teaching each new crop of students. So, too, caring for God's creation is a generations-long task that will go on (God willing) until Jesus returns.

As you take up the work of caring for God's creation, rest assured that it will not be easy work. It is the good work of our times, and it will take many lifetimes. The work of serving God and saving the planet to sustain an unknown number of generations yet to be born gets at the fundamental reason of why we are here.

Consider this question: If God is all-powerful, if God can do anything that God wants to do, and if God wants to get us to heaven, then why weren't we born there in the first place?

Pondering this question brings us to the conclusion that this life, this earth, is a gift from the Lord.

A gift from God is not something to be taken lightly or dismissed as meaningless, disposable, or cheap. So it is right that, as professed followers of Jesus, we should value and fight for that which belongs to the Lord.

I have learned much since *Serving God, Saving the Planet* was written. My view of God and the church has expanded. My love and understanding of the Bible has grown. This past Earth Day, Blessed Earth—a ministry that grew out of this book—convened church leaders at the National Cathedral in Washington, DC. An alliance of seminary presidents came together to sign a covenant to teach, preach, live, and hold each other accountable to biblical stewardship principles. They included the largest seminary in the world, and ones from all around the country. They represented Reformed, Armenian, and evangelical disciplines. They are committed to making sure that the next generation of pastors has adequate training in what the Bible says about caring for creation —one church at a time.

If you are studying this book as an individual or as a congregation, be aware that you are part of a growing movement within the church. I believe that this movement is led by the Holy Spirit —and that it is becoming the most dynamic, intergenerational, and culturally relevant movement of our day.

I wrote *Serving God, Saving the Planet* when I was new to Christianity and creation care. I made mistakes, and times have changed. There are now a half billion more people on the earth than when it was first published. I bought an iPod even though I said I wouldn't. I still dry clothes on the line. I have given up cola drinks (mostly), and my wife and I live in a townhouse even smaller than the home we were in before.

Stewarding God's creation within your world and sphere of influence is a journey. My jaw dropped when a professor and his wife came up to me and said they had given away their 401k after reading my book. "I never said to do that!" I told them. "We know," they said, "but the Lord did."

There is no formula here for the exact size house, car, or lifestyle you should have. That is between you and God. But the one thing I will advise is that you should plan to have your life changed and your faith increased as you study this book.

Best wishes and God bless.

—Matthew Sleeth, MD
August 2012

Chapter 1

Genesis

A few years ago, on a sunny fall afternoon, I sat on a worn granite step just east of Saint Peter's Basilica. I had taken an article written twenty years earlier outside to study. The article, by John Paul II, was an impassioned plea to Christians, particularly wealthy Westerners, to stop harming the environment. Throughout his later decades, the pope wrote repeatedly and prophetically on this theme. His words watered a seed that had been growing in my Western, evangelical heart.

A dozen strides away from me, an ancient woman wrapped in black sat on the pavement with her back against a tall building. Her right hand rested on the ground. She was begging, and she was being ignored. I watched her for a while. An astonishing variety of people passed. Native Italians strolled by, as did a group of men with shaved heads and saffron-colored robes touring from the Far East. Dramatic, dark-skinned Africans wearing vividly dyed cotton clothing walked side by side with somberly dressed Muslims and women in burkas. Then I saw one of the most beautiful sights I have ever witnessed. Three nuns, all advanced in age, subtly detached themselves from the stream of pedestrians. One quietly stooped over and placed money in the beggar's outstretched palm. A moment later, the nun and her friends were caught up in the flow of traffic. The gift was as subtle as a Cold War microfilm handoff. It was done with utter humility, intended to be witnessed by no one.

Seeing a need and acting to meet it is the central theme of this book. *Serving God, Saving the Planet* is a call to individual action. It is a book about the environment written from a Christian's perspective. It proclaims that a problem exists, one as meaningful and real as a sinking ship with billions of passengers aboard. The earth is our ship, an ark for everything that lives. It is the only vessel available to carry humans through the ocean of space, and it is rapidly becoming unseaworthy.

God created the world to sustain all living creatures, and in turn to sustain humanity. He designed this elegant system to function naturally, but our ark of life is changing rapidly. Only a short while ago, my grandfather could drink water from a stream or lake without concern. The fish were not laced with mercury. The water did not harbor dioxin. The air was not yet full of haze. The bounty of nature seemed inexhaustible.

If we had continued in the lifestyle of our grandparents, we would not have the problems we currently face. Our grandparents lived in modest houses, one-half to one-quarter the size of today's homes. They did not travel distances the equivalent of five transatlantic trips annually in their cars. They did not require his and her walk-in closets but could fit all of their clothes in a bureau. A family of seven felt lucky to have one indoor bathroom. Our generation consumes five times more energy per person than my grandfather's.

We have gadgets that existed only in comic books, and yet many people today believe that life without these devices is unthinkable. Which of the items invented in the past fifty years add to our lives, and which subtract? Which enrich our souls, and which only generate background noise? When a church congregation got together for a picnic one hundred years ago, was fellowship, love, or God any less present because the utensils, plates, and napkins weren't thrown in the trash after a single use?

One of the most popular inventions in my lifetime is the computer. For many life revolves around this hybrid of the adding machine, post office, television, movie theater, stereo, telephone, game arcade, shopping mall, virtual community, and more. Research scientists and computer programmers have an axiom — "garbage in, garbage out" — which means that no matter how good or powerful the computer, any answer that comes out is only as worthwhile as the data entered. Our lives are similar. We will come up with good answers only if we ask meaningful questions. The person who begins the day by asking, "What will I wear and how will it look?" may work just as hard as the person who asks, "How can I serve God and save the planet?" It is not the effort put into their actions but the meaning derived from their lives that will vary greatly.

Serving God, Saving the Planet asks the following questions: How can I live a more godly, equitable, and meaningful life? How can I help people today and in the future? How can I be less materialistic? How can I live a more charitable life? What would happen if I led a slower-paced existence? What is the spiritual prescription for depression, anxiety, and anger? How can I become a better steward of nature?

When God called me to this ministry, I was a physician — chief of staff and head of the emergency department — at one of the nicest hospitals on the coast of New England. I enjoyed my job, my colleagues, my expensive home, my fast car, and my big paycheck. I have since given up every one of those things. What I have gained in exchange is a life richer in meaning than I could have imagined. Not everyone can completely change paths, but each of us can periodically examine our lives to determine whether we need a course correction.

Over the past five years, my family and I have made significant lifestyle changes. We no longer live in our big house; instead, we have one the exact size of our old garage. We use less than one-third of the fossil fuels and one-quarter of the electricity we once used. We've gone from leaving two barrels of trash by the curb each week to leaving one bag every few weeks. We no longer own a clothes dryer, garbage disposal, dishwasher, or lawn mower. Our "yard" is planted with native wildflowers and a large vegetable garden. Half of our possessions have found new homes. We are a poster family for the downwardly mobile.

Because of these changes, we have more time for God. Spiritual concerns have filled the void left by material ones. Owning fewer things has resulted in things no longer owning us. We have put God to the test, and we have found his Word to be true. He has poured blessings and opportunities upon us. When we stopped living a life dedicated to consumerism, our cup began to run over. We have seen miracles.

Today I preach about God and his creation. I am one of a growing number of those whom the Lord is using to educate people about his love for them and his love for the natural world. The earth was designed to sustain every generation's *needs*, not to be plundered in an attempt to meet one generation's *wants*.

As I go around preaching and teaching, people share their concerns. It seems that many want a less hectic daily schedule; others long for meaning and purpose, and the security of a rich spiritual life. Still others know what is keeping them from a closer walk with God but cannot overcome inertia to make the necessary changes.

I spoke recently with a group of men. Each described himself as "born again," and yet one told how he could not stop himself from buying cars—cars he cannot afford. Another complained of a persistent problem with credit card debt. A third described the pain —both economic and emotional—of going through a divorce. Being born anew in the Lord is crucial, but spiritual growth must follow. Spiritual growth is a journey we must actively seek.

Getting from point A to point B is not always easy, even if you know where A and B are located. For example, experts tell us that, nationwide, some 50 percent of all adults are overweight. A majority of these folks say that they would prefer to be thinner. As a physician, I can advise every single obese patient how to achieve this goal: Eat less and exercise more. It is that simple. And yet it is not. I doubt there is a publishing house in the world that would print a dieting book—even one that was scientifically proven, guaranteed to work, and written by a doctor of medicine—if all it said was "Eat less, exercise more." The lesson is this: We need to know the thought processes that precede change before we can make similar changes ourselves.

Serving God, Saving the Planet is about getting from point A to point B. It is based on the Bible and my experiences. It begins with an explanation of the problems that result from our lifestyle and looks at the biblical mandate for each of us to be involved in creation care. I share the lessons that most touched and motivated my family to move from thought to action. There are chapters on tuning in to God, and there are chapters on tuning out the world.

Many ask me how my family has made so many changes. Did my kids balk at anything? Yes. Did my wife and I argue about any of these changes? Yes. Have I been hypocritical about anything? Yes, and I will share these experiences with the reader. As much as we all long for a magic pill that will effortlessly transform a family, there is none. Lighting candles, painting designs on our toes, and reciting repetitive incantations have not been responsible for the changes my family has made. True change begins in our minds and in our souls. God gives us the capacity to change. He is the source of all power in the universe.

A few days ago, my wife, Nancy, and I came home to find our seventeen-year-old son, Clark, hanging laundry with his fifteen-year-old sister, Emma. Earlier, he had been weeding the garden while his sister began making supper. This is not unusual behavior for my children in recent years, but the norm. The bickering of their younger days is gone. One "payoff" for adopting the lifestyle changes I advocate is that children and parents work together in a happier, more peaceful home.

The consumer lifestyle demands an enormous amount of work, worry, strife, and struggle by instilling a deep sense of longing and discontent. If all of us were suddenly happy with our homes, for instance, how many decorating magazines could be sold? There is a common belief that 50 percent of marriages fail because people no longer have a sense of commitment or a work ethic. This is nonsense. An average car buyer will sign a six-year loan. Our grandparents would have thought such a commitment insane and walked away. Many today rely on college loans that will take twenty years to pay off. Consumers are willing to make commitments and to work hard, but what are they choosing to serve? A material world or a spiritual world? At the end of a materially rich day, Consumerism says, "Buy more." At the end of a spiritually rich life, God says, "Well done, my good and faithful servant."

I believe that everyone needs to ask, "Is my life, or my family's life, too hard?" If the answer is yes, the solution may be not to work more or "smarter" but to change bosses. In my own life and in my observation of thirty thousand patients, I've seen that working for God and his kingdom has a better payoff than working for the consumer world.

Serving God, Saving the Planet is meant to elicit personal accountability. Its lessons are meant to teach individuals, families, and communities not much larger than a congregation, and yet it looks at larger issues because they profoundly affect each of us. One of our country's greatest problems is our dependence on oil; it affects every aspect of our private, corporate, and church lives. Any material thing of such colossal importance detracts from our spiritual lives, whether or not we acknowledge the dependency.

And yet, global warming may not be the most harmful outcome of our oil habit. When people's lives become dependent on a substance, we call it an addiction. The addictive potential of a substance does not necessarily correlate to the "high" it delivers. A more accurate way to judge addictive potential is to see how willing someone is to go without the substance, or how painful life becomes when it is suddenly withdrawn.

When we are addicted, we tend to start denying or overlooking things. We stop asking questions about where our substance of choice comes from. We fail to question its side effects. We are willing to lower our standards. No one wants a drug dealer for a neighbor—unless, of course, you are an addict.

In *Serving God, Saving the Planet*, we'll look at the moral implications of our fossil fuel dependence, as well as its health effects. What does devoting so much of our lives to obtaining and delivering oil do to us as a country and as individuals? The United States now sends more than $200 billion a year to distant lands in exchange for oil. That means that every man, woman, and child in America is sending about $700 a year to foreign countries just to feed our oil habit. One of those recipients officially forbids religious freedom. Its constitution mandates that the earth is flat. It declares democracy a capital crime. And this country is a major, not a minor, supplier of U.S. oil.

Ours is not the first generation to be morally blinded by building a lifestyle based on energy from foreign shores. Slavery was the importation of cheap energy without regard to its moral cost. States that initially forbade slave energy, such as Georgia, eventually sanctioned it out of envy of the material wealth of their neighbors.

Upon meeting Harriet Beecher Stowe, the author of *Uncle Tom's Cabin*, President Lincoln was purported to have said that it was nice to meet the woman who started the Civil War. Stowe's father was among the northern evangelical ministers who preached against slavery. Other preachers from the south penned equally eloquent *pro-slavery* sermons. The church, like the country, found itself split by the slavery controversy. How could church leaders come to such different conclusions while reading the same Bible? Can we draw lessons from this defining moment in our history, or are we doomed to repeat it?

I have read many of the theological writings advancing both sides of the slavery controversy. The "new commandment" of Jesus —that "ye love one another even as I have loved you"—shows us that one side was right, and one side was self-serving. The proponents of slavery never quote Christ in supporting their cause. Application of this same scripture allows us to see the right side and the wrong side of creation care issues. God and history teach us that we must love those least able to defend themselves, which includes the unborn generations of all species.

Serving God, Saving the Planet asks each reader to take responsibility. Although I believed in the "environmental cause" before I accepted Christ as my Savior, my belief did not translate into action. "They"—Congress or business or anything other than me—were responsible for the insidious poisoning of our globe. I looked at the rate of forest destruction worldwide (one acre per second), the number of species going extinct daily (by conservative estimates, more than one hundred per day), and the loss of blue skies, and I despaired.

After I became a Christian, I went through a process of examining my life. It was filled with sin and hypocrisy. When it came to the area of stewardship, I decided to conduct an assessment and figure out a rough estimate of the actual environmental impact of my family. At the time, I considered myself an enlightened environmentalist. The United States uses more resources than any other country in history, and my crude audit showed that my family used slightly more energy than the average American household. Despite our modest recycling, carpooling, and electricity conservation efforts, we were living an unsustainable lifestyle. We were going about life as if we were the center of the universe, and there was no tomorrow to protect.

This honest inventory is what the Christian faith required of me. How could I say that I was being a good steward when I was causing so much damage to God's creation? How could I say that I cared about my neighbor when the poorest people are most affected by the climate change that I was causing? My lifestyle was not reflecting my espoused concern. I was a hypocrite. After my assessment, I knew my family had to make some drastic changes.

As a Christian, I felt a mandate to align my lifestyle with what I was saying. Seeing the spiritual benefits that went along with our lifestyle changes gave me great optimism. I began to have faith that the church could become a powerful part of the solution to global warming and the degradation of the earth. The environmental movement needed new leadership, and that leadership had to be motivated by moral conviction. I am convinced that when the church becomes fully engaged in the problems of creation care, we will overcome seemingly insurmountable odds. As the thirty million evangelical Christians—and all those who consider themselves people of faith—grow in their understanding that God holds us accountable for care of his creation, we will begin to see positive changes on an unprecedented scale.

This chapter opened with my witnessing a simple act of charity by a nun in Rome. Actions, deeds, and works of charity get heaven's attention. The words spoken on earth that autumn day in Italy are now forgotten. Yet the miracle I witnessed allowed me, for a moment, to glimpse what God sees—our hearts. In that humble gift to a beggar, I heard the trumpets of heaven sound. God's beautiful earth will not be saved by words or good intentions. It will be saved by humble, anonymous acts like turning off the lights, hanging clothing on the line, bicycling to work, and planting trees. People who are grateful for God's abundant gifts, people of faith who are not afraid to be held accountable for care of his creation, will save it.

Chapter 2

An Ounce of Prevention Can Change the World

It was a beautiful fall day in New England, the kind that sends calendar makers running for their cameras. The hospital stood just a few feet from the shore, a brick structure with the added charm of functioning windows. The sight of discreet, white cumulus clouds, the sound of ships' bells and seagulls, and the smell of saltwater drifted in. I was the chief of staff and head of the emergency department, and I was just beginning a twenty-four-hour shift in the ER. I sipped orange juice out of a mug given to me two decades earlier that said, "Trust me. I'm a doctor."

The ambulance crew was wheeling in our first patient, a thirty-two-year-old woman who had a fever and shortness of breath. I parked the mug on the desk, put my stethoscope around my neck, and went over to introduce myself. Sally was undergoing chemotherapy treatment for an advanced case of breast cancer. We talked and I examined her. Where her breasts had once been, she had two purple, diagonal surgical scars. The nurse and I held her sweat-soaked body forward. There in her posterior lung fields, I heard an ominous gurgling.

As we eased Sally back onto the pillows, her husband rounded the curtain with a toddler on his hip and a four-year-old girl in hand. Sally's daughter was excited to give her mother a crayon drawing. Sally took the picture and examined it. Then she leaned over and kissed her daughter, saying, "What a beautiful picture, sweetheart. It's already making Mommy feel better." The little girl beamed in satisfaction, glad that she could help, oblivious to her mother's missing breasts and bald head. With her family in tow, Sally was admitted to the hospital and successfully treated for pneumonia.

A few weeks later, I was on call during a rainy Sunday afternoon when Sally arrived by ambulance again. She was in *status epilepticus*, meaning that she was having continuous convulsions. Her breast cancer had invaded her brain. We worked for three-quarters of an hour, but to no avail. Sally never regained consciousness and died in the ER. During our efforts, Sally's husband had arrived, and he was waiting in a private family room. The nurse and I quickly cleaned up Sally's body, and I pulled out the endotracheal tube. We wanted Sally's husband to be able to see her one last time.

I walked down the corridor and into the family room. Sally's husband looked up at me and knew what I had come to tell him. Nevertheless, it had to be said aloud. "I have bad news," I began. "We tried everything—but Sally died." I took him in my arms and hugged him. "I am so sorry," I said as he began to cry. For a moment he was lost in his grief, and then we noticed his four-year-old. She stood beside us with crayons spread out on the floor. With childish hope, she held out another "get well" picture.

Sally is not unique. In the next ten years, twenty million Americans will be diagnosed with cancer. Twenty million means one out of every fifteen people. The first question you might ask is "Isn't that number a reflection of an aging population?" Yes, in part, but the most dramatic increases in cancers are among children and young people. This is because they are smaller and more vulnerable and have greater exposure to new toxins.

The continual increase in cancer cases cannot be dismissed as a statistical fluke. It is part of a greater problem: environmental illness on a global scale. We should see each new case of cancer as a "canary in a coal mine."

Canaries, small finches with rapid metabolisms, were the companions of miners, always there to warn of the greatest threat: deadly methane gas. Methane—also known as town gas—has no natural color, odor, or taste. The smell you perceive when you turn on a gas stove is added. That added odor allows you to detect a leak or an unlit burner. If miners saw the canary acting funny or falling off its perch, they knew that methane gas was building up in the mine. When the bird went down, it was time to get above ground.

An increase in cancer among pets is another sign that something is subtly and quietly poisoning us. Many of us own dogs and cats that live in our homes and ride in our cars. They drink the same water and breathe the same air as us. The result: they also have skyrocketing rates of cancer. Rover's biggest nemesis used to be a speeding automobile; now it is a tumor. The cancer rates of some "indoor" dogs have tripled in the past thirty years. To date, the reaction of animal doctors is the same as that of people doctors: build more hospitals and offer more chemotherapy, surgery, and radiation treatments. Instead of looking for the cause, we are focusing on the cure. We have forgotten our grandmothers' axiom: "An ounce of prevention is worth a pound of cure."

What caused Sally's cancer? Could it be that our question isn't even the right one? Could it be like walking into a teenager's messy room and asking, "What is the thing that makes this place such a wreck?" The link between some chemicals and diseases is known. In general, there is no such thing as a good red dye. Was it the red dye (that has since been taken off the market) that Sally ate on her birthday cake at age seven that caused her cancer? Was it the dye in the hair color she used when she decided to be a redhead at age seventeen? Was it the dye in the paper plate or the napkins at her college dining hall? Was it the coloring that inconspicuously leached into her skin when she wore the cranberry satin bridesmaid's dress at her sister's wedding?

One of the most toxic red dyes ever formulated is added by the ton to the 6.7 billion gallons of home heating oil burned each year in the United States. Only someone who was suicidal would drink even a small glass of this deadly red dye. Yet it is used without thought—all so that when a wooden stick is inserted into an eighteen-wheeler's fuel tank, it comes out with a red stain if the driver is using home heating oil to fill up his truck. Home heating oil and diesel fuel are the same, but diesel fuel is taxed more heavily. The red dye is used to prevent a few people from using cheaper heating oil in their vehicles. Could it have been the red dye in heating oil that caused Sally's cancer? Will burning more of it to heat our home cause my daughter to fall ill in ten or twenty years?

I have mentioned only one toxic substance that could have contributed to Sally's death. We live in a sea of chemicals. We absorb these poisons and carry them from generation to generation. Currently, more than seven hundred man-made toxins can be found in human tissues. Each new chemical and every pound of exhaust added to the atmosphere is an experiment in just how much we, and the planet, can withstand.

It can be overwhelming to think that heating our homes may be causing cancer in our families, not to mention knocking a hole in the ozone layer over the polar regions. For some, paying for heat and getting through the next month's bills is more than enough to cope with. Many are simply trying to survive, to get by, and to keep their heads above water. "Think globally" sounds great, but there are too many local worries. As an elderly man said to me, "Hey Doc, I'd have to have been living under a rock the past few decades to not've noticed global warming. Everywhere ya look, it's just getting more and more crowded. But what are we supposed to do?"

Turn on an evening newscast. There are stories of hurricanes, tsunamis, melting ice caps, dying seas, war, famine, and mothers who drown their children. With the exaggerated expression of a puppet, the TV reporters frown, purse their lips, nod their heads of perfectly coifed hair in time to prompted words, and tell the story of genocide in Africa or the shortage of "Tickle-Me-Bozo" dolls at the mall. The media entice us with a fast-food diet of sensational-ism, all the while telling us that we are "informed." This stream of news about things "outside our control" leaves us feeling power-less. In one respect, it is consoling to believe that the problems of the world are too big for us as individuals. If they are too big or too complex for us to solve, we are relieved of any responsibility. Powerlessness can be comforting, which may explain our addiction to newscasts and newspapers. As a result, we overlook the dozens of decisions we *can* make every day to help build a better world. Like so much of the news, the story of Sally will probably not stir a reader to action. It may evoke pity, but pity is not going to change anything. If we do not change, if we don't begin to serve God and save the planet, then this book is a waste of paper. Yet, as anyone who has tried self-improvement knows, getting started is hard, and sustaining change is harder. For now, let's just get started.

I frequently hear some variation of the following: "I know there are problems in the world, and we're trying to help. I started recy-cling, but my neighbor throws out ten barrels of trash every week —five of which are aluminum beer cans. How do you keep from getting angry or discouraged? Why are you so happy and upbeat?"

To answer this question, I will tell a story. I have always been a little accident-prone. This, coupled with an active rural farm upbringing and a sense of curiosity, resulted in plenty of child-hood mishaps. Injuring myself, however, was only the beginning of my troubles. Mothers in my world had not heard of ouchless Band-Aids or soothing antiseptics. All households were issued a one-quart, dark brown glass bottle of "methiolade" (also known as Mercurochrome), guaranteed to kill bacteria and burn like blazes. Moms used paintbrushes to apply it to our cuts, scrapes, and road rashes. When we cried or pulled away, they soothed us with prom-ises to "give us something to really cry about" if we didn't settle down.

Perhaps because of the intense pain methiolade caused, or because of the bright red stain it left, or for some other reason, I began to exhibit a violent reaction to the sight of blood: I would pass out. The reaction grew worse as I aged. When I was twenty I tried to donate blood on three separate occasions. Each time I got the feeling that I was suddenly too warm; my vision narrowed to a tunnel; I broke out in a cold sweat; I felt nauseous; and then —boom, boom—out went the lights.

In high school I became a carpenter and built for six years before I went to undergraduate school. One day, I was mortising a door and put a chisel into the tips of my index and middle fingers. As I was sitting on an ER gurney, waiting to be sewn up, I told a passing nurse I wasn't feeling so good. She made a crack about big, strong construction workers and whisked on by. I passed out, hit my head against the bedside stand, and ricocheted off the tile floor. The floor was undamaged, but my head required stitches.

Despite my blood phobia, soon after Nancy and I married I resolved to become a doctor. After two and a half years of under-graduate school, I was admitted to medical school. There was just one problem: My fear of blood had grown to mythical proportions. So, during the first Christmas break of medical school, I arranged to confront my demon. A classmate's father was an obstetrician in Washington, D.C., where we then lived. I arranged to observe a "routine" delivery. This kindly obstetrician knew of my phobia and thought it would be therapeutic if the sight of blood were paired with the joyful arrival of a baby.

I learned much that night. Here's a partial list:

1. There is no such thing as a "routine" delivery.
2. Mothers who have had two previous, uneventful deliveries should quit while they are ahead.
3. A lot of things happen rapidly if normal fetal heart tones just sort of die out.
4. A first-year medical student can and will be recruited to try to push the baby's head back up the birth canal while everyone scrambles to begin an emergency C-section.
5. Once the baby is surgically plucked from its mother's womb, a medical student can pass out on the delivery room floor without being noticed.
6. There is a lot of blood and amniotic fluid down on the delivery room floor.
7. When one wakes up in a large pool of bodily fluids, no further loss of dignity results if one cannot rise to a kneeling position.
8. Side to side motions (similar to those of a salamander) will eventually get a light-headed medical student to the delivery room door, provided the floor is sufficiently slick with the aforementioned fluids.
9. A medical student's pride is not restored when the nurses, nursing students, obstetricians, residents, anesthesiologists,

and ward janitor tell him that, under the circumstances, he shouldn't feel bad about passing out and slithering from the room.

10. Mothers and babies usually bounce back from these traumas without incident.

11. First-year medical students who require sutures in their scalp are not required to pay for said suturing, provided their scalps are split open in the line of duty.

Six years later, I was the senior resident in charge of an emergency room for the evening shift. The facility saw some seventy thousand patients annually. Three critically injured patients had arrived simultaneously from a horrible accident. The situation was so severe that I sent word to the attending doctors for backup, but it would be half an hour before any arrived. One of the victims had lost her left arm. A paramedic brought in the severed limb, and I grabbed it thankfully and gave instructions to pack it in ice in case it could be reattached later.

Over the years, I had jettisoned my paralyzing blood phobia and was now comfortable as a trauma doctor. In this change is the answer to how you can go from feeling overwhelmed by problems to happily working to solve them. The key is to shift from worrying about the problems to becoming an active part of the solution.

Worrying will not keep someone like Sally from dying of cancer. It won't close the hole in the ozone layer. But you and I can become the agents of the cure and jettison our paralyzing feeling of helplessness. We can help ensure that unborn generations will arrive on a healthy planet that needs and welcomes them.

Chapter 3

A Christian's Case for Earth Care

In 2002 the Reverend Jim Ball launched a campaign in favor of fuel-efficient, cleaner, and more modest personal transportation. He was one of the first eco-evangelist leaders to capture headlines with the "What Would Jesus Drive" campaign. Many Christians are unaware of or surprised to find that prominent church leaders from all denominations are calling the rank and file to support clean air, clean water, fuel efficiency, and nontoxic manufacturing. The thirty-million-strong National Association of Evangelicals published a theological document in November 2004 stating that our "government has an obligation to protect its citizens from the effects of environmental degradation." Despite such straightforward statements, the issue of earth stewardship remains divisive among many believers. Why is this? Let's look at some common arguments against personal stewardship of the earth, and then we'll look at the biblically based reasoning that supports stewardship and environmental temperance. Following are some common arguments against stewardship:

"God gave us dominion over everything."

The beginning of Genesis describes the creation of the earth and the teeming creatures on land, sea, and air. It tells of the creation of man and woman and of God's willingness to give humankind responsibility for nature. Contrary to some popular beliefs, one of the first commandments in the Bible is to "tend and watch over" the garden (Genesis 2:15 NLT). Yes, we were given permission to *use* the earth, but not to *abuse* it. As a sojourner on earth, we are entrusted to leave the earth in as good or better shape than when we arrived.

When we drop off children at kindergarten, we cede dominion over them to the teacher. Without this partial transfer of responsibility, chaos would reign in a classroom, and no child would learn to read or write. At the end of the day, when we pick up our children from school, we expect to find them in the same or better condition as when they arrived. We would not tolerate finding them battered or less intelligent at the end of the day. Similarly, dominion over nature does not translate to neglect, license, or destruction.

"But a child is more significant than a tree, ocean, or forest," you might say, and I would agree. So let's consider an automobile for a moment. A car is not alive and, despite advertising hype, is not "made in heaven." Yet I suspect that if we lent our car to a friend (i.e., gave him dominion over it), we would be very unhappy to get our car back dented, dirty, and with an empty tank. Being pro-stewardship is not a case of valuing forests more than people; rather, it means valuing human possessions less, and God's world more. Surely we must value the loan of God's earth at least as much as we value the loan of an automobile, for God's earth is only on loan to each generation.

> God made the heavens and the earth, and his blessings are upon all living creatures.
> And God said, Let the waters bring forth abundantly the moving creatures that have life, and fowl that may fly above the earth in the open firmament of heaven.
> And God created great whales, and every living creature that moveth, which the waters brought forth abun-

dantly, after their kind, and every winged fowl after his kind; and God saw that it was good. And God blessed them, saying, Be fruitful, and multiply, and fill the waters in the seas. (Genesis 1:20–22 KJV)

When the passenger pigeon became extinct, God took note. When we exterminate a species, we forever lose dominion over it. We cancel God's blessings on a species when we destroy it. Furthermore, God placed these creatures at the service of humans, which is to say they are meant to aid and sustain us. When we kill off a species we go against God's dual blessings: We cancel the life God gave to the species, and we forever lose the benefits of that species to humanity. When we ignore a blessing, we show a lack of respect for God. Disrespect is blasphemous. Let us keep in our hearts this thought: God created the earth, and if we do not respect the earth and all of its creatures, we disrespect God.

Indeed, God retains ownership of the earth:

> The earth is the LORD's, and everything in it.
>   The world and all its people belong to him.
> For he laid the earth's foundation on the seas
>   and built it on the ocean depths.
> (Psalm 24:1–2 NLT)

Human ownership is an illusion. How can creatures that die own anything? No matter what you temporarily lay claim to or control, one thing is certain: In one hundred years, you will no longer own it. God introduces this concept to his people early on:

> The land shall not be sold for ever: for the land is mine; for ye are strangers and sojourners with me. (Leviticus 25:23 KJV)

"We don't need to worry about nature; everything will be renewed after the rapture."

The Bible promises that the earth will be renewed; however, this promise has little to do with us now. Why not? When asked, Jesus said that even he did not know when the end would come. Instead, he cautions us to conduct our lives in a way we would not be ashamed of if the world ended today. We must always be ready for the end (Mark 13:32).

Because none of us knows the number of our days, we are to keep the commandments, and love God and all God loves, regardless of how much time is left. For example, suppose we heard that a fiery meteor was going to hit the earth in seven days. Would this news of disaster be an excuse for us to forgo following God's commandments? Would imminent destruction of the earth be a green light to steal, horde food, burn every forest, or ignore the poor?

Those who have no belief in God could rationalize selfish actions out of a "that's all there is" reasoning. However, knowledge of an end time reminds believers to double their efforts to do the will of God. When we pray the Lord's Prayer, we ask for God's kingdom to come to earth. Knowing that God promises to restore the earth is a reminder for us to do our part every day to help. This is how we act out our faith.

"Wealth is God's reward to believers."

God promises to reward his followers, but not with material wealth. He will provide for our needs if we dedicate our hearts and lives to him (Matthew 19:27–30). The problem comes when we confuse our needs with our wants. Time and again Jesus warns of the dangers of having too many possessions. It is not our spiritual longings but our material desires that keep us from a right relationship with God (Revelation 18:13). We are explicitly urged to seek after nonmaterial, eternal rewards.

> Do not store up for yourselves treasures on earth, where moths and vermin destroy, and where thieves break in and steal. But store up for yourselves treasures in heaven ... where your treasure is, there your heart will be also. (Matthew 6:19–20)

"I bought my SUV because it is bigger, weighs more, sits up higher, and is safer in a crash. If I'm going to be in a wreck, I want my family to be safe."

I've heard this line numerous times, which makes me wonder if it isn't on a poster in the back room of SUV dealers. This philosophy is condemned, however, in the Bible. Proverbs 18:11–12 (NLT) says:

> The rich think of their wealth as an impregnable defense;
>> they imagine it is a high wall of safety.
> Haughtiness goes before destruction;
>> humility precedes honor.

If we wish to experience life to the fullest, we may have to do things that seem, well, scary at first. The worldly hunger for permanence and safety "at any cost" is an illusion. It is not a path to God.

> For whoever wants to save their life will lose it, but whoever loses their life for me and for the gospel will save it. What good is it for someone to gain the whole world, yet forfeit their soul? (Mark 8:35–36)

Looking out for number one is not what comes to mind when we recall heroes of the Christian faith. One such hero was John

Harper. Reverend Harper was a transatlantic passenger on the maiden voyage of the *Titanic* and a pastor at Moody Church in Chicago. When the *Titanic* was sinking, Harper gave up his seat on a lifeboat. Later, when he was in the water, he ministered to a young Scotsman. Harper gave his life preserver to save the soul and life of that man. Contrast this witness of love with modern end-zone dances, magazines called *Self*, and SUVs that advertise "Roadway Domination."

"I don't have time to worry about the world's problems. Ignorance is bliss."

Jesus directs his followers to minister to the lowest and least of the kingdom. In the parable of the sheep and goats, he warns that he will deny salvation even to those who call him Lord if they have not cared for the least among society. The "least" includes the naked, the hungry, the sick, the homeless, and those in prison (Matthew 25:31 – 46).

My wife was teaching a high school class and brought up the subject of poverty. One student said that he doubted that anyone in the world today still went to bed hungry. He was wrong, of course, but not alone. A significant portion of our society is so wealthy that we have no exposure to the one billion people who are in a constant state of hunger. This lack of contact with the poor contributes to two problems: ignorance and a lack of perceived opportunity to help those in need. Environmental concerns are intimately tied to issues of poverty, health, and compassion. Ignorance is neither bliss nor an excuse. Ignorance is a route to damnation.

> The discerning heart seeks knowledge,
> but the mouth of a fool feeds on folly.
> (Proverbs 15:14)

Over and over, the Bible reminds us to educate ourselves about the world's problems and then act on that knowledge. We must actively help those least able to speak for themselves—including unborn generations.

"My neighbors all do it. Why shouldn't I?"

When I was a kid, the "Everybody else is doing it" excuse was the single worst reason we could offer when we tried to argue in favor of one of our childish wants. It was sure to be followed by "If all your friends jumped off a bridge, would you jump too?"

The "I'm doing it just because everybody else is" plea was lame when we used it as kids, and it doesn't get any better as we age. Pouring chemicals on the lawn that are poisonous to small animals and children is go-along-with-the-crowd reasoning.

One of the dangers of keeping up with the neighbors is that we haven't aimed high enough. In 2 Corinthians 10:12, Paul says:

> They are only comparing themselves with each other, and measuring themselves by themselves. What foolishness! (NLT)

Jesus is the one to aim for. Whenever we are uncertain about a particular behavior, all we need ask is "What would Jesus do?"

"I'll be dead before the oceans play out or the forests are all cut down."

Selfishness, unlike wine, some cheeses, and Shaker furniture, does not age well. Yet there are people alive today who have lived long enough to see the loss of the American chestnut and the American elm. They've seen the sky turn a purple-gray haze, streams become undrinkable (even unswimmable), wells poisoned, and the death of half the world's birds. After describing these losses, I've heard many sadly say that they're glad they won't be around to see the outcome of another fifty years of business as usual. This group absolves itself of any responsibility for setting things on a better path. It is as if all the little children being born do not warrant an effort or sacrifice on the part of us who are older. Retirement from morality is not mentioned in the Bible; John the Evangelist wrote the last book of the Bible at age ninety while on an island prison.

As Christians, we pray that God's concerns become our concerns —no matter what our age. God is intensely concerned with the needs of the next generation. We who are older and have a greater understanding of the negative changes occurring in nature must be bold.

> The righteous will flourish like a palm tree,
>   they will grow like a cedar of Lebanon;
> planted in the house of the LORD,
>   they will flourish in the courts of our God.
> They will still bear fruit in old age,
>   they will stay fresh and green.
>   (Psalm 92:12–14)

"Tree huggers worship nature. I don't want to be involved with them."

The problem today is not one of nature worship; instead, it is the worship of all things made by human beings. Ask yourself, "How much time have I spent admiring what God has wrought, and how much time am I spending admiring my possessions?" We have hundreds of magazines devoted to fashion, homes, self-image, and cars. We "live" in our cars commuting to and from work and activities. But have you spent an hour in the past week sitting in the woods or a field, enjoying God's creation?

As Christians, we believe that God made the heavens and earth.

He made the teeming animals, birds, and fish. He created the forests and fruit-bearing plants. Heaven is God's throne and the earth is his footstool (Isaiah 66:1). If a person is working to save the Lord's footstool (earth), but doesn't know the owner of the footstool (i.e., an atheist or agnostic), does that mean we should obstruct their labor (stewardship of the created world)?

God prescribes many acts as pleasing to him, among them feeding and clothing hungry children. Not all organizations working to help the poor are Christian. Does that mean that their work should be stopped, or that we should not labor alongside of them?

The Bible repeatedly describes nonbelievers whom the Lord uses to accomplish his will. God instructed the prophet Elijah to be fed by (unclean, unkosher) ravens, and then by a pagan widow in Zarephath. What if Elijah had refused help from these sources? What if he had told God he didn't like the pedigree of his help?

When Jesus asked the pagan woman at the well for water, an opportunity for ministry presented itself. Because Jesus accepted help from a nonbeliever, many in the woman's town came to know Christ. The same opportunities abound for working with nonbelievers in the environmental arena.

I know a Southern family that is in full-time ministry. They describe themselves as living "right where the Bible Belt buckles." They became ill while working in a poverty-stricken area and are now undergoing long-term drug therapy to remove lead poisoning from their bodies. Neither they, nor I, know whether a Christian or a sun-worshiper invented the medicine, but they gladly accept this lifesaving drug. Why, then, would we question the validity of any environmentalist who labors to keep people from getting lead poisoning in the first place?

I am reminded of a well-known tale I first heard as a boy in church. There was a man of faith who lived in a floodplain. It rained hard for two days straight. When the river rose to the man's porch, a large truck drove up in the water. "Get in and we'll take you to high ground," the driver said.

"No thanks," said the man. "I believe in God. He will save me." The truck drove off. The waters continued to rise. A boat came along, and the boatman saw the man in the top floor of his house.

"Get in," said the boatman, "and I will take you to high ground."

"No thanks," cried the man out his window. "I believe in God. He will save me." The boat motored away.

Later, a passing helicopter saw the man clinging to the top of his chimney. The helicopter hovered and the pilot cried, "Grab on and I'll fly you to higher ground."

"No thanks," yelled the man. "I believe in God. He will save me." After the helicopter left, the river rose and the man drowned.

In heaven, the man met God. Obviously the man was thrilled to have made it to heaven. He had only one question: "God, I had complete faith that you would save me from the flood, but you let me drown. Why?"

"That's odd," said God. "I sent a truck, a boat, and a helicopter to save you."

What would happen if the thirteenth-century person for whom San Francisco and Santa Fe are named were in ministry today? Would the media dismiss Saint Francis, patron saint of animals and the environment, as a tree hugger? Would they try to have him thrown out of church because he took seriously God's commandment to preach the gospel to all creatures? Would they insist he undergo psychiatric treatment because he wrote songs like "All Creatures of Our God and King" and "Brother Sun and Sister Moon"? Would they condemn him for penning "The Prayer of St. Francis?"

"Science will find a solution," and the related, "It's up to the government to protect us."

They might, but that hope should be tempered with the understanding that science brought us ethyl gasoline, which was supposed to stop engine knock but gave children brain damage. Science invented spray deodorants to keep teens from sweating; however, these aerosols ate a hole in the earth's protective ozone. Similarly, our government has a mixed record on protecting our health and the environment. To trust that government or science will fix everything is to abdicate our personal roles as stewards. One of the key features of Christianity is its emphasis on a personal God, personal redemption, and personal accountability. We cannot depend on the state, our church, or science to redeem us today or in the afterlife. The Bible says that each of us will stand before God and give an account of our actions—and our lack of action.

"God lives in heaven. Why should we care so much about plants and animals?"

Solomon is known as the wisest person ever to have lived, but he wasn't born that way. After Solomon ascended to the throne, he received wisdom as a gift from God. Many know of his 3,000 proverbs and 1,005 poems, but few are aware that one of his greatest accomplishments was the ability to speak with authority about all forms of plants, animals, birds, reptiles, and fish (1 King 4:31). The wisest human knew that to love God, we must know and love what he loves.

I travel to various churches and enjoy listening to songs of praise. In my lifetime, the method for singing together has changed. Many churches no longer use hymnals and instead project slides with lyrics onto large overhead screens. Behind the song text, scenes of mountains, lakes, forests, streams, pastures, and flocks of birds are projected. But why use these images? Why not use an airplane in the background? Why not pictures of the things we work for, fight for, and own? Would it be wrong to put up pictures of pools, cars, vacation homes, and stereos while singing "This Is My Father's World" or "Awesome God"? In our hearts, we know the answer.

God created the world, and he loves what he created. Read John 3:16 carefully. This beloved verse does *not* say that God loves people so much that he sent his only son to save them. What it says is:

> For God so loved the *world*, that He gave His only begotten son. (emphasis added)

The original Greek text uses the word *cosmos*, and, like the word *world*, the word *cosmos* includes humans but encompasses far more. God loves the world, the whole world. As the song says, "This is my Father's world, He shines in all that's fair; In the rustling grass, I hear Him pass, He speaks to me everywhere."

We live in a time when nature is viewed in a mechanistic way. We say that trees exist to make oxygen, or to give shade, or to be made into paper, and we assign them no further mystery. In other words, nature has purpose and value only insofar as it fulfills our material needs. Our worldview is so mechanistic that we ask questions like "If a tree falls in the woods and no one is there to hear it, does it make any sound?"

The Bible answers this question: If a tree stands in the middle of the forest and is never seen by a human, it has meaning to God. The tree is there to glorify God and to give God pleasure. And yes, if the tree topples over one day, it does make a sound and God hears it. This biblical view is at odds with the industrial worldview, but I find it comforting. Yes, it implies that we have some responsibility for God's earth, but it also means that our God is the kind of God who loves trees, and birds, and flowers. Our God is an awesome God.

The apostle Paul makes an intriguing argument in an appeal to nonbelievers in his letter to the Romans. "Don't believe in God?" Paul asks. "Then get out and take a hike in the woods," he reasons.

> For the truth about God is known to them [nonbelievers] instinctively. God has put the knowledge in their hearts. From the time the world was created, people have seen the earth and sky and all that God made. They can clearly see his invisible qualities — his eternal power and divine nature. So they have no excuse whatsoever for not knowing God. (Romans 1:19–20 NLT)

The Twenty-third Psalm is among the most beloved. Only the Lord knows how many frightened children, people on their deathbed, and soldiers have found hope in its words. It has a power, truth, and beauty that resonate with us a thousand generations after it was written. "The Lord is my shepherd; I shall not want. He maketh me to lie down in green pastures; He leadeth me beside the still waters." Many of us have had our most peaceful, happy, and Godly moments while enjoying nature. There is nothing our twenty-first-century souls cry for like the peace and glory of God's presence.

"A hundred million years from now, humans will all be gone and a new life form will have risen to replace us. The earth will eventually recover from us."

This is most often brought up when I talk with folks who do not believe in God. This reasoning rests on a notion that life is a zillion-to-one bingo game in which the scorecard is cosmic dust and the caller is a series of lucky lightning bolts. Humans, they reason, are a doomed experiment in the game of chance, little more than a replacement for trilobites or dinosaurs. Humankind is no more planned than bad modern art—a hoax of paint randomly splashed on canvas. Because we are an accident, no one need shed a tear at our passing.

If one accepts a philosophy based on the reproducibility of scientific method, then we must state a fact: The earth is the only place in the universe known to have life. Other worlds may have life—but that is an assumption based purely on conjecture. The existence of life defies reason: Life contradicts the second law of thermodynamics and the tendency of all systems to entropy. In our own solar system, the mass of matter that is "alive" (compared to all other matter) is so minute that it is, in a practical sense, immeasurable. Science must accept facts. If we are the only products of a four-billion-year-old game of chance, then what are the odds that luck would again come up with creatures that could write sonnets, ice skate, sing, fly, and laugh?

I, for one, think the home planet is worth fighting for.

I've regularly encountered these arguments against planetary stewardship in discussions with believers and nonbelievers. This list is neither exhaustive nor all-inclusive. Unspoken reasons for neglecting our role as stewards include greed, thoughtlessness, lust, exploitation, and short-term profit. These factors negatively affect our environment as well as our individual walk with God.

"We no longer need God to sustain us. We have science and technology."

From the beginning of our history, humans have known God as both the giver and the sustainer of life. Our ancestors planted seeds and prayed for rain. They thought the sunshine was a blessing, and they bowed their heads at harvest time. They gave thanks when livestock was born. Now, even those who believe in God no longer see him as the sustainer of life. Food comes from a grocery store and clothing from the mall, and shelter is desired for curb appeal.

Our contemporary spiritual unplugging brings a great sense of control. If we are clever and lucky, we can take care of our needs. We all enjoy the fruits of technology. Psychologists and scientists declare us freed from our superstitious shackles: It's foolish to depend on God to send the rain and protect us from the lightning. Yet despite having a record amount of control over our lives, something is amiss.

Ten percent of the women and 3 percent of the men in our country need an antidepressant to get through a day, a day with no fear of starvation, invasion, or want. What's wrong? We find that we can buy a house, but not a home. We can purchase entertainment, but not contentment. We can travel the globe, but we feel utterly imprisoned. We have degrees, but little wisdom.

Perhaps more than any generation, we have rejected the concept of God the Sustainer. If God made nature to sustain us, and if we reject his sustaining gifts, will there be no consequences? I believe that we will have untold misery as we reject God as the source of our lives. As I write this, in our country and around the globe, the weather is becoming hostile. We are having record numbers of hurricanes, heat waves, floods, and droughts in large part because we are abusing God's creation. God planned nature to sustain us. We should work with his plan, but this will require a new mindset.

In October 2004, the Indian subcontinent was flooded by a deadly tidal wave. Such events happen and will continue to happen, but one of the reasons for the record number of fatalities in this case was not the wave but the fact that all the mangrove trees along the shoreline, which normally holds back the waves, had been cut down to make way for the white sandy beaches so loved by tourists.

As we manipulate nature without regard or concern for its underlying design, we will increasingly have to deal with unnatural problems. Diseases that were once confined to the latitude of the Nile River, or the Amazon, are appearing for the first time in temperate zones because of our prodigal behavior. We may find some answers in science and technology, but there is a vast wealth of knowledge and wisdom that can be obtained simply by observing the Creator's methods.

Chapter 4

The Earth Is the Lord's

Just before our daughter Emma's second birthday, we moved into a two-hundred-year-old house that backs up to the Andro-scoggin River in Maine. As we unpacked boxes, our son Clark started itching and feeling uncomfortable. Soon a lovely case of chicken pox bloomed. It was difficult to keep him from scratching in the humid August weather. John, a new neighbor, stopped in to welcome us to the neighborhood. When he saw Clark, John took pity and suggested that he take us down the river in his small boat. Off we went.

Clark was delighted, his affliction soon all but forgotten. "Would you like to try to catch a fish, Clark?" John asked.

"Yes," Clark responded without hesitation. I have hardly fished in my life, but at least I know how to operate a spin cast reel. I put my hands around Clark's, and we cast into the wide, moving river. Almost immediately there was a bite. With a little help, Clark reeled in a black trout. I netted it and brought it up for him to see.

John shouted, "Attaboy, Clark! What a fish!" I clapped Clark on the back.

"Can we take it home to eat?" he asked.

"No, I think we better put it back and let it grow some more," I responded. John gave me an odd look. I'd known him only a few weeks, and I couldn't read his meaning. I released the trout into the water.

Clark cast again. Within a few moments, we had another fish on the line. We reeled it in, and it was practically the same size as the first fish, only slightly smaller. "Dad, let's take it home for dinner," Clark said, clapping his hands. "Let's take it home to Mom!"

"Well, this fish isn't quite as big as the first one, Clark. Don't you think we ought to put it back and let it grow some more?" I queried.

I looked over to John for support. He sat with that funny look, shaking his head; I wondered what faux pas I'd committed.

"I have lived on this river all my life," John finally said, his face melting into a look of awe, "and that is the second biggest fish I've ever seen caught." He shook his head. "You let the biggest one loose a moment ago."

I explained to John that with the exception of a few bluegills caught as a teen, I'd never caught a fish before. The look of admiration on John's face flickered and died. For one moment, he had thought he was in a boat with world-class anglers. Now he knew we were just a couple of lucky beginners.

To Clark's delight, I relented and put the fish in a cooler, and then we headed back upstream. As John and I got the boat up onto the landing, he said to me quietly, "Don't let Clark have more than a few bites of that fish." Then he nodded to a sign warning of dangerous dioxin levels in fish from the river: No one who was pregnant should consume any. Children under twelve should have no more than one fish in a year's time.

Dioxin is a poison produced when paper is made. It causes cancer. And it's like mortal sin; there is no safe level. It makes moms miscarry and children's brains malfunction. So I told Clark a lie, the second and last time I ever lied to my son: I drove Clark home, and then I went to the grocery store to swap our fish for a nontoxic one—which shows how dense I can be. How did I know the fish I bought didn't have more mercury, PCBs, or dioxins than the fish I threw away?

What we call "nature" isn't the same nature our great-grandparents knew. Even if they lived as far south as Baltimore, they could cut eighteen-inch blocks of ice off ponds in the winter to cool their food in the summer. Now, thanks to global warming, we don't get enough ice up here next to the Canadian border to do that.

Today my family lives on the Connecticut River in New Hampshire, sixty miles north of Dartmouth College. Dartmouth was founded to counter the liberal trends in Boston colleges, so it's surprising that Dartmouth was the site of one of our nation's first college protests. Students had finally grown tired of the kitchen workers plucking forty-pound salmon from the Connecticut and serving them day in and day out, week after week. Now there are plastic bottles and tires in the Connecticut, but no salmon.

Similar stories abound nationwide: No chestnuts on Chestnut Street, no elms on Elm Street, and soon no maples on Maple Street. In 1880, the residents of New York City alone ate half a million passenger pigeons. What if they had stopped to think before they "spent" the whole species? The great auk, the caribou, the blue pike, the parrot owl, and the Carolina parakeet are the tip of a melting iceberg of God's creation. They are gone forever. There is nothing that can be done about these vanished species, except to learn from our mistakes. A family on a tight budget must be more careful about how it spends its limited income. As a society, we have far fewer natural resources in our "account" than our predecessors. We need to be more careful stewards or we will leave our children a legacy of malls, big-box stores, highways, houses, and

—worse—potential catastrophe resulting from global warming. If people of faith have no concern for the future, who will?

You might ask, "What's so important about the natural world?" In seeing tens of thousands of patients, I've gotten an idea of what kinds of work people enjoy and what kinds they truly love. Those who work under the open sky are in love with their work and are the most resistant to giving up their lifestyle. Family farmers will hang on by their fingertips. Fishermen will go out to sea taking great physical risks for almost no monetary reward. I once had a man come in after pulling his lobster traps. His left hand had gotten caught in the power winch, which cut off his little and ring fingers. He threw a bandage on and continued pulling traps for two hours. "Just stitch me up so I can get back out again, Doc," he said. His life was the water. What made him love it so much that he hardly noticed pain?

Another waterman told me, "You don't know what it's like to be out there. When you kill your lights and engine, you're alone with God Almighty. The seals come alongside, and you can see clouds of plankton lit up by the phosphorus they make. The whole Milky Way pops out at you. When you turn your head, you're looking down the center of our galaxy! I'd do anything not to lose my chance of being out there with God." Perhaps it is not by accident that Jesus first called fishermen as disciples; I can hear Peter talking similarly about crossing the Sea of Galilee at night.

The place where the land meets the sea holds a special allure for humans. A majority of the world's population lives within a dozen miles of shoreline. I wish that every person who wanted to could make a living from the sea; fishermen, clam diggers, lobstermen, shrimpers, and urchin divers—like hunters on land—often have the greatest love and knowledge of the local environment. The longer I lived near the water, the more I loved it.

People may deny that we are destroying nature. They may believe that oil will flow from the ground forever. They may convince themselves that humankind does not need to change fundamentally, or that they have no responsibility for the future. But I have noticed one barometer of society's health that few can deny: Depression is on the rise. I hear it and see it everywhere. We live with more and more material goods and wealth, and yet a deep sense of anxiousness is in the air. A sadness blows through our culture, and no one seems to have a handle on it. Secular and Christian self-help books fill the shelves. Five percent of school-aged children and teens are diagnosed with clinical depression. The symptoms cross the boundaries of class, race, and faith.

Sadly, many Christians are ashamed of these feelings. They believe that their witness will be undermined if they share their sadness. They wonder, "Why does God allow me to feel this way? Why don't I have the enthusiasm of others in the church?" They pray, and they feel no peace. They go to worship, and the joy soon fades. They experience loneliness in the body of Christ. Some make heroic daily resolves to overcome these anxieties and sad feelings, but the effort seems enormous. "When will it get better?" they wonder. Many take an inventory of their lives and see a loving spouse, children, material blessings, and security. They say to themselves, "I have no right to feel this way while others are starving." The empty voice of despair is always knocking at the door. They drive themselves to read the Bible and devotionals, and they beat up on themselves when they fail to respond as they think they should. Another sermon about Job will not set them right.

How do I know these people? I'm a doctor. People share their pain with a physician because they are looking for answers. I, too, have had these feelings. What can we do? We can look for lessons. Sometimes we can learn something about one disease by looking at another. In this instance, we can begin to understand feelings of depression by examining diabetes. Sounds odd, I know, but stay with me.

Good doctors begin the examination of diabetics as they would a small child, by approaching their feet first, not because an adult needs to be coaxed into trust but because many diabetics can't feel their feet. Diabetes leaves a certain percentage of sufferers with nerve damage. As a result, they feel no pain.

What happens when diabetics can't feel their own feet? They don't receive a warning that something is wrong: If a splinter or an ingrown toenail results in an infection, the diabetic may have no pain signals to tell him to seek help. As a result, diabetes is the leading cause of foot loss in our country. Leprosy acts similarly in the hands. People mistakenly think that lepers lose their fingers from the bacterial infection. Not so. It is the numbness of the fingertips that causes so much harm. Pain can be a blessing from God.

Depression is mental pain, a signal that something is wrong. It may be caused by multiple factors, but the bottom line is that pain is a symptom, a warning signal. When I began practicing medicine, the only drugs available to treat depression had immediate and hard-to-tolerate side effects. "Simple depression," our psychiatry professor taught us, "runs a predictable course. If left untreated, over 90 percent of patients will have relief of symptoms in six months." At that time, physicians balanced the risks of untreated depression with the risks of antidepressant drugs. For many, it was safer to wait out the depression or to change unhealthy lifestyles than to risk the drugs.

Then new drugs came along with far fewer and less dangerous side effects. The trigger point of beginning drug therapy was lowered from "Are you feeling suicidal?" to "How are you doing at work?"

Today it's common for patients to be on antidepressants for years. Many have tried to get off but have been unsuccessful. Has the nature of depression changed over the past few decades, or are more Americans depressed because we are ignoring a message that God wants us to hear? When God instructs his people, does he send pain to get them back on track?

Before we get to some of the answers, let me share the results of a very informal survey I've conducted over the past fifteen years. It sheds some light on just how far we've strayed from God's positive message, and from the uplifting power of the world he has created for us.

"I have a hypothetical question for you," is how I begin my survey. "I have a time machine. It will take you anywhere in time you choose to go. Wherever you go, you will be safe. You will speak whatever language you need to and will have whatever money or currency you need. You will be gone for one month. Wherever you go, you may choose the specific socio-economic group and situation you wish to live in. However, if the place you choose has a system of injustice, you are not allowed to make changes. When the machine returns you to the present, the only things you can bring back are your memories."

And off they go. Older people tend to choose the recent American past, such as the 1950s. Folks in their forties often choose America before Columbus. Youngsters whiz away for a month to romp with dinosaurs. For a reason I've not been able to puzzle out, women who identify themselves as feminists head for Paris during the French Revolution. If you choose ancient Egypt, it will be overrun with other time travelers. The answers are fun, and people enjoy thinking about this hypothetical kind of question. Carefully re-read my instructions, and choose for yourself where you would travel.

Out of the hundreds of times I've asked the question, only a few times have folks answered "the future." The future is an optimistic and logical answer, for it is the only place where we can pick up things of real value. We could bring back the cure to cancer or the secrets of fusion power. We could warn mankind of disaster. The three people who chose the future did so for just these reasons.

But why does nearly everyone choose the past? Is it because something about the past is less scary than the future? What would my study have shown if I'd asked the same question two hundred years ago? I think that most would have chosen the future, just like the author of the Declaration of Independence did. Whatever his faults, Thomas Jefferson carried the words of Christ in his coat and read them daily. He faced his beloved house, Monticello, toward the west, toward the future and the vast wilderness. Jefferson, Adams, Franklin, and Washington all expressed in their writings an optimistic belief in the future.

One of the textbook features of depression is a lack of interest in — or a fear of — the future. One gifted psychiatrist I had during training put it this way: "Ask patients what they see themselves doing a year, five years, or ten years in the future. If they start rattling off answers, they aren't depressed." The more depressed a person becomes, the more shortsighted they are.

My informal survey points to a society-wide pessimism about our future. Current public health statistics point to the same conclusion. Our forefathers saw the glass half full; we see it half empty. What does the Bible say about depression? Does it offer a solution?

The Twenty-third Psalm, recorded three thousand years ago, says the Lord restores our soul by leading us to streams and pastures. In the 147th and 148th Psalms, we are taught that the Lord will heal our broken hearts; he calls each star by its name; he makes the rain fall and hears the cry of a hungry blackbird. He sends

THE EARTH IS THE LORD'S

snow, and frost, and cold, and wind. Beasts of the field praise him, as do the sun, moon, fish, timber, and fruit trees. God has created cattle, insects, and robins to praise his name. "He hath also established them for ever and ever: he has made a decree which shall not pass" (Psalm 148:6 KJV).

For three thousand years, believers understood that the world was created and sustained by God. This truth was known to Maltbie D. Babcock when he wrote the beautiful song "This Is My Father's World" in 1901:

> This is my Father's world, and to my listening ears
> All nature sings, and round me rings the music of the spheres.
> This is my Father's world: I rest me in the thought
> Of rocks and trees, of skies and seas;
> His hand the wonders wrought.

We increasingly live in a man-made world, and that world is making us ill. When the psalmists advise us how to heal spiritually, they do not tell us to purchase a television, car, house, self-help book, or exercise equipment. God, they say, is to be found in the natural world that he created, a world filled with the grandeur, beauty, and peace that are so often lacking in our material world.

What remedy does God prescribe for our souls? Still waters and green pastures. Find a place where there is nothing man-made in sight. Sit or lie down. Be still, and know who God is (Psalm 46:10). Do not pray. Do not worry. Do not think. Your house, your cell phone, and your new kitchen do not give glory to God. The Bible states that if it is God-made (streams, mountains, birds, trees), it praises God. "Praise ye him, all his angels: praise ye him, all his hosts. Praise ye him, sun and moon: praise him, all ye stars of light" (Psalm 148:2–3 KJV). When only God-made things surround you, you are in a fellowship of praise.

If you live in a city, try to find one small area that consists of only God-made things. If you must, lie on your stomach and stare at a one-square-foot area. If there is noise or highway sounds, put your hands over your ears. You will hear the sound of your own pulse and breath. That's okay. And that's the point. You are God-made. We have forgotten that we have far more in common with a honeybee than we do with our SUV or DVD.

While teaching a group of local youths in Vermont last week, I passed around a picture of a Hummer. Out of three dozen teens, all but two could immediately identify it. Then I passed around a large sugar maple leaf. The sugar maple is the most common hardwood broadleaf tree in the northern forest, the source of our local maple syrup, and the symbol of the country a few miles north of us. Only two students could identify the leaf.

Perhaps many of our problems, including those of depression and anxiety, are warning signals that we are living a lifestyle that God does not sanction or want us to lead. The response to mental pain and discomfort should be to seek restoring connection with God. In seeking quiet moments, green pastures, and still waters, we may find just what our soul needs.

Do you know in which direction the Milky Way traverses the sky? As the phases of the moon progress, does the light go from right to left, or left to right? Can you identify a greater number of trees or cars? If the Bible says God knows every flower and bird, why do we spend so much effort knowing the names of man-made items? Maybe we're paying attention to the wrong things. Maybe this is why life seems so hard. If this is our Father's world, maybe we should pay more attention to it.

Chapter 5

Moving from Faith to Works

What good is it, my brothers and sisters, if someone claims to have faith but has no deeds? Can such faith save them?... As the body without the spirit is dead, so faith without deeds is dead.

— James 2:14, 26

A decade ago, I would have told you that our family was concerned about the environment. I would have said that we were true "conservatives," working to preserve nature. That was talk. We have progressed from talking a good talk to walking a better walk. How did we go from saying we were concerned to actually making a difference? When asked by pollsters, 90 percent of Americans identify themselves as "kinder than average." If we say we care about the least in the kingdom, if we identify ourselves as "kinder than average," if we see ourselves as responsible stewards of nature, then we are content. Contentment does not result in change.

The content mind is one of the greatest obstacles to a rich spiritual life. The content mind is a proud mind. It has nothing to learn; it has an answer to everything and no more questions to ask. Jesus wants us to have an active mind, like a child's, full of questions. Jesus taught in parables, simple stories even a child could understand. This is one reason he says we must be like children if we are to gain entrance to God's presence — because a child is still capable of learning.

None of Jesus's parables is better known, more retold, or harder to enact than that of the Good Samaritan. Jesus is prompted to tell this parable by a man who wants to know exactly what he needs to do to get into heaven:

> On one occasion an expert in the law stood up to test Jesus. "Teacher," he asked, "what must I do to inherit eternal life?"
>
> "What is written in the law?" [Jesus] replied. "How do you read it?"
>
> He answered, " 'Love the Lord your God with all your heart and with all your soul and with all your strength and with all your mind'; and, 'Love your neighbor as yourself.' "
>
> "You have answered correctly," Jesus replied. "Do this and you will live." (Luke 10:25–28)

Thus, Jesus boils down the life-giving aspects of religion to (1) love God with all your heart, soul, strength, and mind and (2) love your neighbor as yourself—a code for living in sixteen words. In the Gospel of John, Jesus again points out the central importance of loving our neighbor as ourselves. In John 13:34, he declares the Golden Rule to be "a new commandment."

In our story from Luke, a religious attorney believes that he has Jesus trapped in a technicality because, in the strict letter of Hebrew law, the term *neighbor* may apply only to someone of the same religion (Leviticus 19:18). Jesus tells the lawyer the parable of the Good Samaritan to teach that the spirit—not the letter—of the law is what God wants of us:

A Jew is traveling from Jerusalem to Jericho when he falls among thieves. He is then robbed, stripped of his clothing, beaten, and left for dead on the roadside. As he lies groaning, a fellow countryman happens along. He is a priest from the temple, and he passes by without breaking his stride. Next a Levite comes down the road, crosses over to look at the beaten man, and then continues onward. We might pause here and ask, "Why two men passing by without helping?" Jesus is the master of descriptive economy; why not tell the tale with just one uninvolved sojourner? I believe that Jesus is illustrating the continuum of our responses. The priest doesn't even admit or acknowledge that there is a problem. The second man has compassion or some understanding of a problem. He probably crosses over and says, "What's this country coming to? Why don't they do something about the highway safety?" But what does this passing thought do for the unconscious man? What do a hundred or a million compassionate thoughts accomplish?

Jesus then describes a Samaritan who comes down the road on a donkey. Samaritans were a group looked down upon by Jews of the day. Nonetheless, this Samaritan takes pity, and his pity moves him to action. He gets off his donkey and helps the roadside victim. He binds his wounds, clothes the man, lifts him onto the donkey, and takes him to an inn. When the Samaritan leaves the following day, he pays the bill for the Jew's room and board. In addition, he promises to cover any additional expenses until the man fully recovers.

"So which of these three do you think was a neighbor to the man who was mugged?" Jesus asks.

The lawyer cannot bring himself to say "the Samaritan" and so responds, "He that showed mercy on him."

Christ then says, "Go and do likewise."

Love God and love your neighbor as yourself. Who is our neighbor? We are commanded to love those who might not believe in God, be conscious, have a voice or political power, or have the ability to thank us. Further, we might be required to keep on supporting them even after we part company. Loving them might entail personal risk or sacrifice. Finally, it might make us look foolish or even disrespectful to our friends, church, and family. In Jesus's time, the Samaritan would have been the object of scorn or ridicule if it became known that he had aided a Jew.

Love thy neighbor as thyself—one cannot claim to be a Christian and ignore the Golden Rule. It isn't a suggestion or a guideline; it is a commandment from God. What is the connection between the parable of the Good Samaritan, the Golden Rule, and the environment? Isn't our choice of homes, cars, and appliances just a matter of lifestyle, and therefore not a moral or spiritual matter? Does God care whether I drive an SUV, leave the TV on all night, or fly around the world skiing? The Bible doesn't mention any of these things. They didn't exist in Jesus's time. Yet Jesus taught the spirit of the law, not the letter. From the spirit of the law, and from the example of his love, we can determine the morality of our actions.

Reading and pondering the parable of the Good Samaritan has resulted in the greatest spiritual insight I have had, an insight that has led to personal action. Spirit and action is a dualistic state and, as such, resembles the commandment to love God and our neighbor. Jesus instructs us on the nature of God. God is in heaven. God is a spirit. We cannot know God through incantations or rituals. Therein lies our dilemma. We are physical beings; what can we do in a physical sense to worship a spiritual God in heaven? He is a unique God, this God that Jesus teaches about. Unlike Zeus, Athena, Baal, and the other gods of AD 30, this God actually loves us—all of us. Remember that we said one couldn't love God and fail to love what God loves? Well, he loves us, and so we must love us. Because God is a God of perfect justice, he loves all of us equally. Good parents don't play favorites, and neither does God.

God loves all of our neighbors—the ones we don't like, the ones we don't know, and the ones yet to be born.

God created the earth. He made it to be self-sustaining and renewing. Throughout history, the natural world has fulfilled its role. It has carried a thousand generations largely without the help or consideration of humans.

When I speak in a church, I bring along a case of efficient lightbulbs to give to people. I refer to the Energy Star website (www .energystar.gov) which urges us to consume less energy. Formed by the Environmental Protection Agency under George Bush Sr.'s administration, the Energy Star program appeals to our sense of patriotism, logic, and brotherhood. It says that if every household changed its five most used bulbs to compact fluorescent lightbulbs, the country could take twenty-one coal-fired power plants off-line tomorrow. This would keep one trillion pounds of poisonous gases and soot out of the air we breathe and would have the same beneficial impact as taking eight million cars off the road. A decrease of soot and greenhouse gases in the air translates into people who will be spared disease and death. Some sixty-four thousand American deaths occur annually as a result of soot in the air. Throughout my childhood, I knew of only one schoolmate with asthma. Now on a hazy day, dozens of kids in every school reach for inhalers to aid their breathing. God did not design the air to make us short of breath. It was meant to sustain us.

The Harvard School of Health looked at the impact of one power plant in Massachusetts and found that it caused 1,200 ER visits, 3,000 asthma attacks, and 110 deaths annually. Nationally, the soot from power plants will precipitate more than six hundred thousand asthma attacks. These are just numbers, albeit large ones. For me, those numbers boil down to one young girl early in my medical training.

It was a triple "H" day in the nation's capital—hazy, hot, and humid. A dome of smog hung over the city and extended far beyond the capital beltway. The weatherman told those with illnesses to stay indoors, but eight-year-old Etta Green and her brother went to a neighborhood playground. I began my afternoon shift in the ER wing of the children's hospital while Etta and her brother were running through a sprinkler to cool off. As Etta exerted herself, her airways began reacting to the smog. The muscles that line the bronchioles of her airways involuntarily contracted, while the mucous cells began a pathologic overproduction of thick fluid. Within a few seconds, this fluid buildup became what we call an asthma attack.

Etta's brother ran back home for her inhaler, and bystanders called 911. Within a few minutes, a rescue unit was on-site and began treating and transporting Etta. They radioed ahead that things were not going well. To one side of the ER, we had a room with eight beds set aside specifically for asthma cases. On that afternoon fifteen children occupied the area—receiving oxygen treatments, inhaler treatments, and IV medicines. The growing anxiety of the EMTs in Etta's ambulance made it clear that she was too ill for this area. A nurse flipped on the lights in a trauma room, and we assembled there.

The doctor in charge of the team called out what he wanted everyone to do. I was given the job of intubating Etta, if needed. The ambulance crew arrived. She was being "bagged," meaning that the paramedic was trying to oxygenate her with a mask over her mouth and nose and an Ambu bag that forced air into her lungs. Her thin, limp body was quickly transferred to our trauma gurney.

Etta's pulse was ominously slow, and her oxygen saturation

level was barely readable. The Ambu bag was hard to compress because of the resistance in her clogged airways.

"Matthew, go ahead and intubate. Tammy, get an art [arterial] line in; I want her paralyzed too," the leader called out. I lifted Etta's small hand and held a few endotracheal tubes next to her little finger. Then I selected the one closest in diameter to her finger, a trick I'd been taught for quickly getting the correct size. I paused a second to lean down and whisper in Etta's ear, which is the only way to communicate with a patient in a crowded, noisy room.

"Etta," I whispered, "I'm Dr. Matt. I'm going to put a tube in your mouth and get you breathing right." I looked into her frightened eyes. "I'm not gonna let anything bad happen to you, sweetheart," I promised. Her left hand still rested in mine, and I thought I felt a weak squeeze.

Two images from that scene still haunt me. The first was her little finger held next to those plastic endotracheal tubes. That hand was so small and vulnerable in my oversize palm.

The second image came thirty seconds after I intubated Etta. The team leader yelled for quiet. He held his stethoscope on her chest. "Give her a breath," he ordered, and I squeezed down on the bag. Etta had on a bathing suit the color of a fluorescent green hula hoop. Pictured on its front was a happy, smiling whale blowing a spout of water into the air. Etta must have loved that bathing suit. One couldn't help but smile at the frolicking whale. Trying to lift that whale by forcing air into her lungs is my second haunting memory. Despite the rescue squad, and despite the best efforts of an entire pediatric emergency department, I broke my promise to Etta. She died of air pollution on that summer day.

No recent event has had a greater effect in bringing out the church's leadership in defense of the environment than the proposed Clear Skies Initiative legislation. The title "Clear Skies" is

Orwellian language. Orwellian language (so named because of the language used in George Orwell's *1984*) is when one says one thing and means another, sometimes the opposite, for the purpose of manipulating perceptions. We've become so used to Orwellian terms that we forget that *life* insurance is really paid at *death* and that medicine for the *sick* is called *health* care. So the National Association of Evangelicals mobilized to stop the *Clear Skies* legislation. Why? Because it was a bill to increase air pollution. Even its proponents admitted that it would result in four thousand more premature deaths annually. Imagine if all politicians were bound to state their case in straightforward language. Would anyone stand up to support the "More Pollution, Greater Death of Citizens, All for Increased Profits and Short-Term Gain" bill? But that's what the Clear Skies Initiative was about.

It is tempting to point to a self-serving lobbyist or a power-hungry elected official and blame him for one of the sixty-four thousand annual deaths from airborne soot. But what about me? What about us? Remember the lightbulbs? By changing lightbulbs, hanging clothing on the line, taking fewer trips to the mall, carpooling, and owning more modest homes, Christians can save lives — not statistical lives but little children like Etta. They can save their own grandchildren and, just as importantly, the lives of people they will never meet.

Christ teaches us about a continuum of conduct. In the Good Samaritan parable, we see three distinct sets of awareness. The priest represents the first. He represents no awareness, no action, and no ability to think abstractly. Next, we get the Levite who crosses over and looks at the mugged man. He is aware that there is a problem. What keeps him from acting? There are two factors. One is fear, or the lack of courage to carry out one's convictions; the other is hypocrisy, or knowledge without action. Knowing enough to say "that poor mugged man" or "poor little Etta" and not doing something to help (like changing your lightbulbs or carpooling) demonstrates hypocrisy. If pride is the father of sin, then hypocrisy is its mother. "Remember, it is sin to know what you ought to do and then not do it" (James 4:17 NLT). To get to action, one needs faith. Faith results in a convicted heart—a heart that is not proud.

The priest is a content person, and by inference, a proud person. At the other extreme, the Samaritan is far less content. This is why we are asked to take an inventory of ourselves when we come to Christ. It isn't just to make ourselves feel inadequate—although that is certainly one result. It is to make our hearts grow. We become less fearful, and more capable of doing the Lord's work. What is the Lord's work? It is taking care of the least in the kingdom, such as the unconscious traveler, or Etta, or generations not yet born. If the Samaritan had come along just as the thieves were ready to attack and yelled, "Hey you, what are doing? Get away from that man!" would he have been any less pleasing to God? Preventing harm is as important as repairing it. At the beginning, middle, and end of every day, the Samaritan is less content with himself, and less complacent, than the priest.

Another dimension of a servant's heart is to recognize opportunities for service and to act on them. Thousands have heard the parable of the Good Samaritan and resolved to help the next wayward traveler that they happen upon. But the opportunity to help abandoned, unconscious human beings, like asthmatic children, must often be sought out. We can wait a comfortable lifetime to serve unless we put ourselves in a position to help.

A number of years ago, I was invited to address a group of physicians on the topic of "How to Avoid Malpractice." I began by asking the doctors to write down their last clinical mistake. "Just jot down quickly what comes to mind. Keep it anonymous. Don't write your name or the patient's." A typical note said something like "failed to check potassium level on diabetic in-patient." This was all done very rapidly. "Let's just keep moving," I instructed. "Now fold your paper in half even if you didn't write down a mistake, and then when it's folded, put a check mark on the outside if you've ever been involved in a malpractice suit. Now, fold it again and pass it to me," I said.

Nearly every paper with a "malpractice check" was blank on the inside. In life, as in medicine, people who cannot call to mind their last mistake are most likely to make another.

As a doctor, I benefit from remembering the last mistake, or even all the mistakes, I've made. One of the greatest mistakes we humans make — one that we all make daily — is the sin of hypocrisy. Recall the last ten times you were hypocritical. Can you recall? Hmm.... Can you recall even one time you acted in a hypocritical manner?

When I first heard the poll in which 90 percent of Americans said they were kinder than average, I wondered about the other 10 percent. My first thought was "The 10 percent who actually go ahead and say that they aren't kind must be really mean." But upon further reflection, I realized that in that 10 percent reside those who are truly the kindest. It is people such as St. Paul who identify themselves as the very worst of sinners who represent the true heroes of the faith.

One hot day last summer as I came into the kitchen to fix myself a glass of ice water, our daughter Emma took a cookie and popped it into the microwave for a few seconds. I had never seen her do the cookie-warming trick, and I commented, "Emma, don't you know that it takes energy to heat up that perfectly edible cookie?" She responded, "What about you, Dad? Don't you know that it takes energy to cool down that perfectly drinkable water?" She then thought better of her tone of voice and started to apologize. "No, you're right," I admitted, though my pride was wounded. And she was right. It is so easy, so tempting, to point out the hypocrisy of another, while overlooking my own.

Everyone is fairly good at seeing the shortcomings in other people, churches, movements, governments, and countries. There is certainly plenty of hypocrisy among environmentalists. I was invited to visit a woman who writes about the effects of fossil fuel consumption. I pulled up to her rural Maine home one day. Two SUVs were parked in the drive. The Maine house is one of three that she owns. All are heated year-round, and she complained about the $2,500 she had spent heating this house the previous winter. "We kept the heat turned way back, and we were here only on weekends," she said.

As we talked, I thought to myself, "May the Lord save us from well-intended, wealthy environmentalists who want to save the planet." One of her SUVs puts fourteen thousand pounds of greenhouse gases into the air each year. My hybrid puts out three thousand pounds a year. Our family of four spent only $550 for energy that year. My feelings of smugness and pride grew. I thought that if she didn't change as a result of her own research and writing, how could she expect someone else to change?

The problem with this kind of thinking is that I'm comparing myself with a person of my choosing, and so I make myself feel good. While I was visiting, the writer talked disparagingly about people who drove Hummers, and I suppose the drivers of Hummers compare themselves to people who "thoughtlessly" fly everywhere, and in turn, those people feel pretty good about themselves because they don't own their own jets.

To move from thought to action, we must feel some discomfort with who we are. We will not develop any discontent if we compare ourselves to people who behave more selfishly than ourselves. If I compare myself to someone whose sole source of transportation is a bicycle, then it's tough to feel smug about the three thousand pounds of gases I put into the atmosphere driving a lavish hybrid automobile.

Compared to a family in the coastal town of Massade, Haiti, whose annual income is $540, who eats only two meals a day, and who cannot buy its way out of the effects of global warming, how thoughtful am I? What kind of a neighbor am I? The 1 1/2 tons of greenhouse gases my hybrid car produces contribute to the change in sea level and the fish populations on which they depend. Comparing myself to my neighbor is useful, but to which neighbor? In Jesus's parable, the Samaritan compares himself to the mugged man. He applies the Golden Rule, and he is compelled to act.

Jesus relentlessly tells his listeners to observe the plight of their less fortunate neighbors and take steps to help. Christ asks us to change our behavior. In order to change, we're going to have to have some benchmark to know what our behavior is. What is your behavior toward God's creation?

Most of us are not able to walk down pathways we have planted with trees. We do not know how many pounds of trash we have plucked out of streams. We have not composted our yard waste, much less eradicated an invasive species of algae from a pond. For the majority of us, our relationship to the created world is not one of caretaker or steward. Our typical reaction to nature is to not see it, or to see it only when a vacation or a sporting activity takes us into contact with it. It is sobering for me to admit that I can identify more species of automobiles than trees.

Are you kinder than average in your treatment of the earth and your neighbors? In order to move from thought to action, you will have to recognize that some action is needed. For actions in which there is no universal right or wrong, it can be helpful at least to be aware of what others are doing. We may think ourselves philanthropic and generous until we see a widow giving away her last two pennies.

When we are truly grateful, we give God thanks for our blessings. When we are ungrateful or feel a sense of entitlement toward material blessings, we tend to ignore or not give thanks. Many of us give thanks for our food. We know that farmers have worked hard to produce it, and that God has provided the sun and rain and wind vital to the harvest. We bow our heads in prayer and thank God for our food. Few of us recognize, however, that people work, fight, and die to bring us energy.

Energy—electricity, wood, coal, gasoline, propane, and oil— is like food. It is a blessing, and it sustains us. Our relationship to God's gifts can be one of entitlement, ignorance, and gluttony or one of praise, thanks, and temperance.

When was the last time you bowed your head in thanks when filling your car with gasoline? If you haven't done so, is it because you don't think it is a blessing? Do you feel entitled to fill up? Is home heating oil something God or the world owes you? Do you feel you should have all you want, and at the price you want?

If they were here today, who do you think would be more likely to say a silent prayer of thanks at the gas station—the priest or the Good Samaritan? Which one would be more likely to worry about the effects of his lifestyle on others? Who would change the lightbulbs to save lives? Are you, like the Samaritan, ready to move along the path from ignorance to awareness and from compassion to action?

Chapter 6

Too Much Stuff

"How many of you are rich?" I asked the sixth-grade class. The twenty-three youngsters looked around at each other and laughed, and a few chimed in, "Not me!"

"I mean, how many of you are from wealthy families compared to the rest of the world?" I clarified.

Everyone in Mrs. Doland's class was in agreement. No one was from a wealthy family. The Cedar Woods Elementary School I was visiting was located in a semirural town with prosperous farms and light manufacturing. All the kids were well dressed and fed.

"How many of you live in an apartment?" None did.

"How many of you live in a house your parents own?" All the hands shot up.

"How many of you have a car—okay wise guys, how many of you have parents who own a car?" I queried.

All the hands shot up.

"A computer?"

Same response.

"A television?"

"We've got two!" was countered by "We've got three."

It turned out that all but two had flown in an airplane. I explained that only a tiny percent of people living on the earth had ever been in a plane.

These children are all "rich" by world standards. At the point at which people have their own home, enough food to eat, clothing to wear, running water, a sanitary sewage system, a television, a computer, and the ability to ride in an airplane, they are in the top 20 percent of the world's inhabitants.

When I asked who they thought was rich, many rattled off the names of television characters and sports stars. They already had internalized a belief system that will leave them forever struggling. I asked what toys they owned, and a cornucopia of products was named. More enthusiastically, they called out the names of possessions they hoped to own in the future. Possessions represent many things for us. Offered as a gift, they may be a sign of someone's affection. They may ease boredom, provide transportation, impress others, or give us physical comfort. But they all come with a cost. The purchase price may be just the beginning—thanks to the miracle of credit payments.

Children's books and songs acquaint us with consumer logic. Take the song about the old lady who swallowed the fly. Most of us would say, "Stop!" Instead this witless gobbler swallows an arkful of creatures; she swallows a horse, to stop the cow, to catch the goat, to catch the dog, which she swallowed to stop the cat, to catch the bird, to catch the spider, which she swallowed to catch the fly that she initially ingested.

Sounds loony? If she had only stopped when it was just the fly she'd swallowed! Yet too many of us have purchased the table saw to build the shed to hold the utility shelves that organize the badminton set used twice a year at the family picnic. Allow me to illustrate from life.

Todd was one of the most technically talented emergency physicians I've ever known. He was tall and dark and had the square jaw of G.I. Joe. He and his wife lived in the "starter" home they'd bought when they first came out of residency. Since then, they'd had two daughters. Even though each daughter had her own room, they began searching for the "perfect home on the water."

Todd's wife, Angie, would drop by the ER with real estate sheets on homes under consideration. I looked one over and asked Todd, "What's wrong with this house? It looks pretty, and it's on the water."

"No, we went to see it. The house is nice, but with the leaves on the trees, you can't see the water. And if you're going to live on the water, you might as well be on the water," Todd clarified.

The process continued for a year and a half. Houses on the water were fetching more than they had anticipated. During this time, Todd began to pick up more and more shifts. Sometimes he'd finish a twenty-four-hour shift at our hospital only to dash off to work at another facility. He was ramping up his salary so they could qualify for a larger mortgage. As Todd began working all over the state, he needed to buy a new car, and then a cell phone to keep in touch with Angie.

"Todd, what about this house?" I asked as I looked over a data sheet left on the desk. "It's right on the water. You can see the ocean in the photo."

"Do you see any dock in the picture?" he asked.

"No, but you could put one in."

"The realtor took us to see the place at high tide," Todd explained. "But I found out that it's on a mud flat most of the time."

The local coastline has high and low water varying by some eight to ten feet. A deepwater shoreline—one that falls off rapidly—was what Todd and his wife decided they needed. They found a likely candidate only to realize they were on the eastern side of a peninsula. "Sunsets, that's what Angie enjoys," Todd said.

At last they found a home at the end of a peninsula with a deepwater dock. There was only one problem: the house. "It's a mess," Todd proclaimed. They consulted an architect, who was able to salvage part of the garage but otherwise designed a whole new dream home for the site. Todd worked more hours trying to offset the skyrocketing costs of construction. In January, he was so exhausted and the family was arguing so frequently that they threw caution to the wind and went on a lavish, tropical island vacation. Todd returned with a tan and a frown on his face. He related more arguments as the winter and building project progressed.

By spring the house was complete. Todd came to work one day in a rage. His wife had gone on a shopping spree and spent nearly $20,000 on curtains, rugs, and furniture. They had built a home too big for their old furniture, she explained. In retaliation, Todd went to a boat dealer. "No sense in living right on the water if we don't own a boat," he reasoned. The boat dealer sold him not only a boat but two Jet Skis as well. No payments were due until the winter. When Todd hauled his new boat home using his wife's minivan, he burned out the transmission. So Todd and Angie bought a large SUV with a towing package and leather seats. When they arrived home, they were chagrined to realize that the one part of the old house they'd saved—the garage—wasn't big enough to hold the new SUV. The architect and builders returned, and in a matter of weeks the garage was rebuilt.

Todd and Angie no longer live in the dream home on the water. When they got divorced, the lawyers grabbed a third, and they each walked away with half of what was left. If they had only stopped when it was just the fly they'd swallowed! The chicken, the duck, the goat, the mouse, and the kangaroo could have warned them: Don't let Thing One and Thing Two into the house, whatever you do.

We can watch a similar script played out every day, in every town and city throughout the country. The divorce rate among Christians is the same as among non-Christians. And the conflict most often cited in divorcing couples is money. But is the conflict money or unrestrained consumption? Which would have done Todd and his family greater good: having more money or wanting fewer things?

We had too much stuff in our previous home. By making a few phone calls and writing to a central clearinghouse, Nancy has been able to stop almost all the mail-order catalogs we once received. But one company would not take the hint. On its pages you'll find headlines like "At last! An automatic golf ball washer!" It has a product that once made me pause. No, I'm not talking about the robotic vacuum, the massage recliner, or the ionic wind machine. I'm talking about the product that says, "Finally! No more missing keys!"

The device that's guaranteed to make life easier is a small transmitter with tiny receivers that can be placed on your keys, wallet, or other "misplaced" articles. Press the button on the transmitter and your lost glasses start beeping, allowing you to locate them. I contemplated buying this device, dog-eared the page, and left the catalog open on the kitchen counter.

Because I've always been somewhat absentminded, the ability to instantly locate my wallet, keys, or a pair of scissors would certainly simplify my life. Scissors! I decided to cut out the ad and put it in my pocket. I opened the drawer—but where were the scissors? Those kids! They were constantly taking off with the scissors. The week before, Nancy had bought a packet with four of them. I recruited my daughter, Emma, and we began looking for a pair.

Together we searched fruitlessly for five to ten minutes. I knew there had to be four new scissors hiding, and any number of old pairs. Nancy and Clark arrived at that moment. I explained what was going on. Nancy began checking the same places I had. "If we don't find some, I can always get another pack," she said, trying to placate me. By now I had started my "when I was a kid" spiel. You know, "When I was a kid we had only one pair of scissors. Well, my mom also had pinking shears, but we weren't allowed to touch them! If we didn't put the scissors back when we finished using them, we went on bread and water rations for a month! You kids are so spoiled!"

The problem with this kind of communication is that the kids usually roll their eyes, or the mother interrupts the dad, or one of them brings the bike in for the children before it gets rained on, or goes and buys more scissors. And nothing is learned. This brings up one of the most disturbing causes of materialism: bad parenting. More than one family has purchased a new vehicle with multiple rows of seats to keep two unparented children from fighting.

I sat down and looked again at the ad for the "Finally! No more missing keys!" Then I pondered: What will happen when our family gets so many things we misplace the transmitter? Will we buy a tracking device to locate the transmitter to find the keys we are missing? "At last! A GPS-assisted robot" to locate a tracking device lost when looking for the transmitter that finds missing keys. And so on.

We buy things for many reasons: to cheer ourselves up, out of guilt, to reassure ourselves of our worth, because we cannot discipline our children or ourselves, and to try to make our lives more meaningful, easier, or interesting.

On no subject is Jesus more clear than on materialism: a life focused on possessions is a poor and misguided life. Over and again, he urges us to seek a spiritual path and a life of loving one another. It may not be technically impossible to get to heaven if one is rich, but it is nearly so, he warns. Real treasures do not rust, run low on power, become obsolete, clutter up closets and garages, or rack up credit card debt. One need never worry about a real treasure being stolen. Real treasures are never hoarded. They are shared.

It's one thing to know what's right, and it's another to do what is right. As Ludwig van de Rohe said, "God is in the details." By the time most of us realize that our possessions own us, they, well, own us. Getting rid of them is not easy. How much is too much to own? I cannot tell you. I sometimes bring a cardboard box to lectures. Inside are all the pens and pencils I could find in our home. There are hundreds—a lifetime supply for ten families.

Simplifying means having less, wanting less, being satisfied with what you have or less than what you have. It does not mean boredom. People with too many things are the most easily bored. St. Francis owned only his robe, yet was never melancholy or bored. Owning less does not mean you will be without friends, or even admirers. If friends like you for your car, house, or furniture, what kind of friends are they anyway? Maybe it's time to make new friends.

All diets should start with a weigh-in. Take a stroll around your abode. Open the drawers and closets. Do you have a basement, attic, garage, spare room, or storage unit? How many items do you own? Do you need 100 ... 1,000 ... 10,000 ... 100,000 items to live?

Just take the garage or basement and count every single item. Too many to count? Start with your closet or the drawer of your desk. Begin to get rid of things you don't use, because if you don't use them you don't need them. Have a yard sale and give the money away. If you haven't worn it in a year, let it go. Someone needs your cast-offs now. Giving them away three or five years from now will not clothe a poor person today.

As you see your place "open up," as you decrease the number of things you own, don't go out and get more! My grandmother had hundreds of axioms. One of them was "If you think you want something, wait a month." One of three things will happen if you follow this sage advice. One: You will forget. Two: You will no longer need it. Or three: You will need it more. Most often, numbers one and two will happen.

Next, borrow and lend. All over New England where I live, thousands of canoes sit high and dry in garages and basements. I live on the Connecticut River—Canoe Central. During the summer months, a dozen canoes may pass by on a Saturday. This means that thousands of canoes are waiting for use in garages. If you don't own one and feel a desire to go for a paddle, borrow one. If you own one, make sure folks feel comfortable coming by and getting yours. If people don't feel comfortable borrowing your "stuff," you need to change. If you don't feel comfortable borrowing from your neighbor, maybe you need new neighbors. How are we going to live together forever in heaven if we can't even share a chain saw?

Getting rid of things allowed our family to move to a smaller home. As my kids look around, they are beginning to ask for an even smaller house. We are currently on another round of divesting ourselves of things. This time, we're letting go of things that we had previously decided we could not do without. The old windup clock from my uncle is nice. It has sentimental value, but my uncle is gone. Is it more important to my dead uncle to have the clock sitting on my shelf or to sell it and give the money to our missionary friends, to Samaritan's Purse, or to Sustainable Harvest International or to purchase vitamins for the people of Honduras? I can think of only a few reasons why God would want me to log on to eBay. Selling the set of china from a grandmother or an unused, old camera and using the money to feed one of his children is right at the top.

Our family's relationship to things is changing. It makes everything easier. Stores selling clothing or electronic gear are places that hold no sway over me. I love music, but until my current system dies or can no longer be repaired, I'm set. I'm not convinced that the music that sounded good on a record sounds any better on eight track, cassette, CD, or mp3. I'm not swallowing the iPod fly, nor am I buying the whiz-bang tracking device. In fact, now that we've given away so many possessions, I can always find the scissors.

Whenever I am tempted to buy something, I ask myself, "Will it bring me closer to God?" The average person is exposed to three thousand advertisements a day through radio, TV, newspapers, bus signs, billboards, Internet, magazines, and store windows. Many of us have access to cash or credit. What will we buy? Our culture shouts and screams just one thing: consume. How do we resist the world's cornucopia of goods, services, and merchandise when we are told by every input, both conscious and subconscious, that there is some *thing* that will make our lives just a little bit better, fuller, or more convenient? How do we resist the temptation of a laptop that is 5/8 of an inch thinner than the one we currently own and were thrilled to own twelve months ago? Haven't we denied ourselves a giant-screen TV … or a flat-screen LCD … or a plasma-screen TV long enough? What's the harm of one more pair of shoes to go with the new dress bought last week? And what about a purse? After all, the right pocketbook is needed to match the shoes bought to match the new dress.

Where is God in all of this consumer rumination? If you haven't found God at home, will he be more likely to inhabit a vacation home? Remember when the disciples and the crowd gathered on the hillside to hear Jesus speak? Remember how before Jesus began to teach, Peter got up and read the good news announcements? Those who had kids that needed to be carpooled to a soccer game were excused. And remember how they announced the tool sale at the superstore? Recall how they said that only a fool wouldn't tear out Formica countertops and replace them with granite ones? Remember how they suggested buying pearls and jewelry at a "great price" even if you needed to charge them? Afterward, Jesus preached "saving" *and* investing in the famous Sermon on the Amount. You don't recall this? There is a reason why you don't.

The Christian is not at liberty to do whatever he likes. Christians are constrained by conviction to think about their lives, their actions, and their responsibilities. One of the litmus tests for a decision is: Does this action, saying, movie, etc., bring me closer to God? The more this question is entertained, pondered, and posed, the closer to God the Christian will find himself. When "Will this _____ bring me closer to God" is carefully considered, you will find that what is good for the environment often coincides with the "yes" answers. The times that the question is answered "I want it," "I need it," or "It would make *me* or *my* family happy" will most often coincide with a worldly decision.

While it is true that we cannot all live as St. Anthony did, it is equally true that we can all start to live more like Jesus.

There are some very good books that describe ways to live more simply, lessen our impact on the created world, and avoid the prison of consumer debt. Among these is *What Can I Do?, 50 Simple Things You Can Do to Save the Planet*, *The Tightwad Gazette*, and *Your Money or Your Life*. Check them out from the library and read them. Later in this book, I will go over some of the areas where change had a major positive impact on my family's bottom line—both our bank account and our impact on the environment. Some of the areas that I mention may not have a big economic effect but will help in your walk with God.

Always keep in mind that when a Christian does any activity, he is to shine as a light to the world. Have fun and enjoy; don't get legalistic. The path toward responsible stewardship is analogous to having a bunch of friends who are smokers who know that you used to smoke. If you are humble about having quit, you'll find your smoking friends asking for your advice. If you appear smug or holier than thou, you will be a positive witness to a party of none.

We exist in a living, created world in which the Bible tells us that God knows every scale on a fish, every hair on our head, and the flight of every sparrow. We are to aspire to all things godly; therefore, it would be wrong to go through life in an unthinking or uncaring way. Similarly, we are not to ruminate or worry excessively. Try to keep a balance and harmony, seeking in all things to grow closer to the joyous bounty that God has provided in his natural world.

Chapter 7

An Hour of Work,
A Day of Rest

Mark Twain defined work as "what you are obliged to do." Magazines and travel brochures tout the importance of rest, but honest work is just as vital to our lives. Without it we become ill. Let's extend Twain's definition. Work should accomplish something real, something positive, and stress our muscles. Therefore, the definition of work does not include what I'm doing now—sitting at a desk. If I got up and pedaled an exercise bike, that wouldn't fit the definition of work either, as it accomplishes nothing tangible. In our world, real work as I'm defining it is becoming scarce and is given little or no societal value.

There is less and less work—labor that we are obliged to do, and that is real, positive, and physical—in our jobs. Most have to look for work of this sort at home. Yet our culture is obsessed with labor-saving devices. With all this effort to do away with work, one might get the idea that work is unhealthy.

As a physician, I believe that the opposite is true: that without real work we develop serious problems. I'd noticed the positive benefits of meaningful physical work in my patients' lives, but until recently, I had only what scientists would term anecdotal evidence. To draw real conclusions, one would need to study the health of a large group. From some patients in the ER, I learned about one such case study.

George and Ginger were taking time away from their jobs. They had been married thirty years. Both worked for large psychiatric hospitals. Each had spent decades caring for severely ill patients who required long-term hospitalization. George worked in a facility that treated those classified as criminally insane, while Ginger worked in a long-term hospital for those without criminal records.

I met them when they came to our coastal area to vacation and to do some fishing. As I walked around the curtain, the two of them were seated together on a gurney, and two charts rested on their rack.

"That's right, Doc. We're a doubleheader. You see, I'm hooked on my wife," George laughed. And indeed he was. A fishing lure with three sets of triple hooks joined them. Ginger had initially hooked herself on the lure, and when George tried to extricate her, she jumped reflexively and snagged him.

"Bet you've never had one of these. We're such klutzes," Ginger chimed.

"Well, you're the first *married* couple I've seen attached to each other," I answered.

"You're kidding, Doc. You mean you've had other people hooked on the same lure?" George asked.

"You'd be surprised. I had one guy with his hand caught on a lure attached to his friend's forehead. I've taken apart people who were glued together and pneumatically nailed together—even twin brothers who had their fingers stuck in the same pipe," I said.

We chatted about these cases as I opened a workbox of ordinary household tools. I took out a bottle of small corks and started sticking them on the remaining exposed barbs. "And because I've had to separate an ER doctor from a patient he was injecting, I put these corks on the exposed barbs *before* I inject you with lidocaine." Sixty seconds later I had them free.

"George, do me a favor," I asked.

"Sure, Doc."

"Step over to this scale." He looked puzzled but went along with me as I weighed him. "Thanks," I said. "I just have to fill out some paperwork and I'll be back."

I filled out the charts and then pulled out one of my "big game" fishing certificates. They say:

On this _____ day of _____ month in the year of _____, _____ caught a _____ lb. Trophy. Certi-fied by Dr. Sleeth, _____ Hospital.

I brought the certificate back and presented it to Ginger. "Usu-ally I just weigh people who've caught themselves, but in your case you really bagged a trophy." They laughed, and we chatted some more. Then a serious look came over Ginger's face.

"I wish our hospitals had the sense of humor that yours does. They changed regulations this past winter, and all the joking has stopped," she related.

"Same thing at my place, Doc. We're both under the same state regulations. It killed off patients in both our hospitals. We lost more of our folks over the winter than had died in the past four years," George added.

"You're making this up," I said. "I know bean counters are heartless, but you mean they outlawed humor?"

"No. They made it against the law for our patients to do work," George began to explain. "After that, the fun went out of so many of the patients' lives. They just died." It seemed that some well-intentioned person objected to patients having chores if they weren't paid for their work. The meaning of many of these folks' lives was not in the craft groups or in watching television but in the routine daily work they did. For most of them, this consisted of making their beds and cleaning their room. For some, it was helping with cooking or laundry. None of the institutionalized persons wanted to stop doing their "jobs." But regulations are regulations, and they were physically prevented from working.

Their story was confirmed by two subsequent visitors I had in our hospital. How could anyone be so cruel as to take away the meaningful routine of an institutionalized person?

Many of us have built lives in which we have neither rest nor work. Our jobs do not stress our muscles and joints. Our rest is a series of events in which we give our minds over to machines such as televisions, computers, and DVD players. We use machines to chop vegetables, brush teeth, wash our dishes, and record our thoughts. But what is the cost of saving ourselves work?

All labor-saving devices use electricity or gasoline, cost money, produce heat, and make noise. Why do we love them so? What happens when we stop using a manual lawn mower? The nonmotorized variety is inexpensive and quiet and uses no fossil fuels. The push mower requires us to exert energy; thus, we obtain exercise and become healthier. By its very nature, the manual mower dictates a reasonably sized lawn. What happens when we decide to save labor and purchase a gas-powered lawn mower? It spews out poisonous fumes, which we inhale. The mower is loud and damages our hearing; mowing our lawn requires little effort, and our muscles atrophy.

Reason, restraint, and the virtue of temperance disappear. Our lawns grow to a size associated with a few megalomaniac old-world monarchs. We laze, sleep, eat, and drink more. Finally, when we gain too much weight, we drive a two-ton vehicle to a health club where we can pay to work against the resistance of a machine. Why not just back up and push our own mower?

Physical work gives us health and meaning. While the disciples sailed, Jesus walked across the Sea of Galilee to meet them. He picked grain. He washed his disciples' feet. Work was not beneath him. He thought no physical labor was undignified. The washing of feet is a sign that God is willing to stoop low and to work to save us. For millennia, men and women have used simple manual labor as a way to connect with the divine qualities of Jesus.

We have unconsciously taken work out of our lives. If we want work back, we're going to have to consciously reinstate it. Let's use drying clothes as an example. The standard electric dryer consumes energy at a rate of 5,000 watts, meaning that it takes five kilowatt-hours of energy to do one load of laundry. If your family dries one load of laundry a day using an electric dryer, you use 150 kilowatt-hours of electricity a month. Back at the power plant, one ton of poisonous gases is created each year to run your family's dryer.

When our family initially stopped using a clothes dryer, we did so because we no longer wanted to produce poisonous gases. Now, we live in a house with no dryer. Clothing dried in a machine lasts only half as long as line-dried garments. The "lint" you pull out of the trap consists of fibers shredded off your clothing. Now we save money, have clothes that last longer, and aren't polluting as much. But those benefits are the minor benefits. What we discovered was the dignity of work, and the spiritual fruits of doing it in a monastic manner. What do I mean by this?

St. Anthony is cited as starting the monastic way of life in AD 270. He sold his belongings, gave the money to the poor, lived alone, read the Bible, and did manual labor. He did this in order to grow spiritually. When I hang the laundry, I make it a spiritual event. I pray, talk to God, and sing gospel songs. I pair a minor physical task that requires little thinking with a dialogue with the Creator of the universe. I may occasionally resent hanging laundry, but how can I regret time spent with God? The same goes for shoveling snow, hand-washing dishes, chopping vegetables, or biking to the post office.

All honest work can be done for the glory of God. As time passes and we grow in our understanding of God and the uniqueness of this planet, we reject more and more "labor-saving" machines. There is an old saying: If you are troubled, chop wood and carry water. This is wise advice. If you pray at the same time, so much the better. Begin to build an hour of work into your daily life. The result will be more life in your day.

The flip side of work is rest. God commands all of us to take a day of rest each week, but how many of us take his advice? Imagine you're at work on a busy day. You haven't had a break all morning, and then your boss walks up and says, "I want you to take off the rest of the day."

"Are you sure?" you reply. "It's pretty busy. Have you got someone to take my place?" you ask hesitantly.

"Don't worry," the boss answers. "I'll cover things for you."

"Are you sure?" you ask. "Because I can stay a while."

"No," the boss says, "I just want you to take the day off and relax."

"Wow, thanks," you reply.

You gather up your things and hurry out. As you exit the door, your boss calls to you. You knew this was too good to be true. "Just one more thing," he says.

You turn and reply, "What?"

"I want you to know that it's not just today I'm talking about. I want you to take this day off every week. There's only one condition," he adds.

Your stomach tenses. "What?" you query.

"I'll give you this day off permanently. Just promise me you won't work, not even around your house. Okay?"

You take a full nanosecond to think this through. "No problem! You've got a deal!" you shout as you head home to relax.

How many of us have a boss this generous? How many would turn down such an offer? We may not have a CEO this considerate, but our God is.

Five thousand years ago there were no appliances, no grocery stores, no telephones, no immunizations, and no toilet paper. If the rains didn't come, the crops failed. Yet people haven't changed. People in ancient times struggled with the same problems that we struggle with today. When I first read the Old Testament, I wondered, "How can they call this a loving God?" Yet, the more I have studied the ancient scripture, the more loving, timeless, and compassionate God appears. In the midst of all the turmoil and struggle, he tells us to take off fifty-two days a year and rest. The Sabbath isn't just a divine invention; it's a sublime gift.

Taking one day a week for a Sabbath celebration is a great way to maintain our spirit and relax. Like many Americans, I grew up with a "no work" Sabbath that fell on Sundays. It was part of our culture. I enjoyed it, and then I lost it. However, I never forgot it. It's like a smoker who remembers the year when he quit or the woman in debt recalling the time it didn't loom over her. A Sabbath is that good, and it can be any day of the week.

I'm not proposing a legalistic holiday. What I have "rediscovered" are the benefits derived from taking one day a week and setting it aside for spiritual renewal and rest.

When was the first Sabbath? No one knows. Calendars have changed radically over the ages. In the early Roman world, the week consisted of eight days, and the length of a year varied widely. The longest known year occurred in 46 BC and lasted 445 days. Rome later adopted the solar calendar that we still use today. The much older Hebrew and the more modern Muslim calendars are based on lunar cycles.

Despite having no relationship to any celestial occurrence, we still use the seven-day week introduced to us in Genesis. The sanctity of the Sabbath day is established and then further reinforced (Exodus 16:22–30) until finally, in chapter 20 of Exodus, it is carved in stone as the fourth of the Ten Commandments. The fourth commandment is the first law on the planet establishing a code of conduct between master and slave, host and guest, man and beast. It is the longest of the commandments and offers a rhythm of work and rest, whereby all creatures may synchronize with the Creator's divine week.

> Remember the Sabbath day by keeping it holy. Six days you shall labor and do all your work, but the seventh day is a sabbath to the LORD your God. On it you shall not do any work, neither you, nor your son or daughter, nor your male or female servant, nor your animals, nor any foreigner residing in your towns. For in six days the LORD made the heavens and the earth, the sea, and all that is in them, but he rested on the seventh day. Therefore the LORD blessed the Sabbath day and made it holy. (Exodus 20:8–11)

One of the surest bits of evidence that God really exists and that the Bible is true is the repeated failure of humankind to get things right on its own. As the writer and theologian C. S. Lewis said, anything made by man starts up and runs for a time and then sputters out. This applies to our businesses, our governments, and our religious practices. The Sabbath was God's gift to his people. Then people got involved. They started adding laws and subclauses and exclusions. From the time of Moses to the time of Jesus, the Sabbath of God digressed to legalistic game playing.

Here's an example of a legal "loophole" in the area of travel: I want to go to Joe's house, which is four thousand paces away. The Pharisees decreed that walking more than two thousand paces constitutes work. To get around this, I put food under a rock two thousand paces in Joe's direction. When I reach the food, I'm legally "home" and can "begin" a two-thousand-pace walk to Joe's. This was an actual way of circumventing the Sabbath rules at the time of Jesus.

Let me recount a story of legalism in my own family. It was a late afternoon in July when Clark (who was four years old at the time) came running out of the house we were renting and into the attached barn. As he flew past me, his little voice yelled and faded with a Doppler shift, "Emma is trying to bite and hit me!" The screen door of the house barely had time to slam before it was catapulted open again by Emma (who was two years old). Her blond curls were windswept, and her legs carried her little body with wild determination. Emma had no eyes for her parents. All she could see was her brother's receding back. As she bolted past, I swooped down and picked her up in the crook of my right arm. Nothing about her face altered, and her arms and legs continued to pump as if she were still on the ground. "Emma!" I yelled. "Why are you trying to bite and hit your brother?"

Her pistoning arms and legs halted. She turned her head toward mine. Her face reflected the countenance of the innocent, the falsely accused; and then, just as quickly, a look of righteous indignation overtook her. She stared into my eyes and shouted, "I am not trying to bite and hit Clark! I am only trying to bite him!"

By slavishly and concretely observing the Sabbath, the Pharisees of Jesus's time missed the point of the fourth commandment, just as two-year-old Emma missed the point of "no hitting." Oh, how the maker of heaven and earth, the fountainhead of all truth, knowledge, and love, must groan when we act as concretely and legalistically as a two-year-old.

When we fail to understand the spiritual side of a message, I fear it is because we have not developed the language that God speaks. Think of a day of rest as an opportunity to practice the language spoken in heaven. It is not English. The life of rushing about, of getting and spending, impedes our ability to learn the divine language.

Most of us habitually hurry. Our schedule rules us. If it isn't our schedule, it's our children's that has us going seven days a week. Even if we say we could personally commit to a Sabbath day (it can fall on any day), our children need to be driven to this or that activity, birthday party, or sporting event. Thus we teach our children our priorities. If we are compelled to transport them seven days a week, we are teaching that sports or activities are more important than God. Our job as parents is to lead, not follow. We, who are old enough to have lived in a culture that once took and gave a weekly day off, can find answers and a model to recapture something good.

When I was a child, commerce stopped on Sundays. The animals had to be milked and fed, but no one put up hay on a Sunday. Folks didn't mow grass, shop, or travel, except to nearby relatives. Following Sunday school and church, we walked home and shed our dress clothing. Many families had a ritual chicken supper in the afternoon. Afterward, our parents staggered toward couches and beds in a food-induced soporific coma. Children were free to walk or bike to each other's farms and do what we wanted, as long as we observed the commandment to "keep the noise down." This meant that playing catch was okay, while a pickup game was out of bounds. The grown-ups' attitudes mellowed on that day of rest. I recall the change in their moods as well as our wonderful freedom to daydream or read books. Somewhere in the back of my mind, the mental-health benefits of a predictable rhythm of work and rest, activity and quiet, were established.

By the time I had my own children, I hadn't celebrated or observed a Sabbath day for more than a decade. Sunday had grown into America's second biggest shopping day. When I became director of an ER, I had another doctor do the monthly calendar, and she scheduled me to work most Sundays for a twenty-four-hour shift. As I got to the age of forty, these shifts took more out of me, and it took me longer to recover from them. Somewhere along the way, I decided to stop doing "work" around my house on Saturdays in an effort to shepherd my strength for the next day's shift.

My first "rule" was no shopping. I find that I can pray or meditate for hours and have that peaceful glow taken away by ninety seconds spent in a retail establishment. The one time Jesus displays anger and indignation concerns shopping (John 2:14). This is when Jesus drives the merchants from the porch of his Father's "house." Commerce can interfere with our worship.

A wonderful thing happens when we repeatedly come to rest. We have time to think. I found God on my Saturday afternoons, or perhaps it simply got quiet enough for me to hear him once again. I found God by returning to the Sabbath, as did my son, daughter, and wife. Not bad for merely following a millennia-old custom. Stop work and find God.

Our day of rest was initially nonreligious, but it resulted in me having the time to contemplate the big questions in life. I believe that there are forces that would keep us so busy that we never have

SERVING GOD, SAVING THE PLANET

time to live, and that God designed a day of rest to keep those forces at bay. We confuse working with living. One of the truest bits of advice I've heard around the hospital is that no one comes to the end of life and complains, "Gee, I wish I'd spent more time in the office."

The focus of our Sabbath day is much more spiritual than it was years ago; nonetheless, I still need to remind myself to "chill out" and read a book or watch the passing clouds.

If the thought of a day at home with no work, television, shopping, or projects sends you into an antsy sweat, you are hooked on busyness. Time to shake the habit. Start with half a day, or even an hour, but start.

What qualifies as work for you? You get to decide. For me, driving is work, writing is work, and reading a newspaper is forced hard labor. Some of the things our family does on the Sabbath are resting, relaxing, listening to music alone and as a family (same for reading), meditating, talking, thinking, listening, walking, reading the Bible, sleeping with the Bible propped on chest, praying, going to church, and helping others. All of the Lord's activities can take precedence over rest. Teaching, preaching, healing, and care of the sick, the hungry, and those in prison may, and have, interrupted my day of rest. But I still think it is beneficial for the family to take a weekly "time-out."

Nancy enjoys her long Sunday prayer walks. Emma and Clark avoid schoolwork; they will cram in work the day before in order to preserve their day of rest. In many ways, youth have more pressures to conform to a seven-day workweek. It is especially important to show your own personal desire for a Sabbath and then support your children in the same. I tell the kids to let me play the heavy, i.e., "We can't go 'cause Dad says so."

The people who must work on Sundays or lose their job often

fill the lowest-paying positions. A person manning the line at a fast-food restaurant frequently is paid minimum wage and given no benefits. This is exactly the type of worker who was previously protected under the Ten Commandments and hundreds of years of Christian tradition.

It may not happen for a time, but imagine if once again everything came to rest on Sundays. We could use 10 percent less foreign oil. The skies would be cleaner and quieter. As with our family, I believe many others might be led to "still waters" and God.

God is the creator of quiet and rest. God is love. God is good. Hurry, bustle, and noise are bad. God did not create them. Who would you like to have for your boss: the creator of quiet and rest or the maker of hurry and noise? You get to choose, at least one day a week.

Chapter 8

Television:
More Real Than Real

The first TV my family owned was a cast-off from my grandparents. It was a large, heavy black-and-white unit with variable reception and reliability. Frequently my father would remove the back cover and hunt among a glowing, alien city of vacuum tubes, searching for one that was dark. He would drive the five miles to town to a tube tester at the Western Auto Store. The salesman would plug in the dark tube, confirm its nonfunctioning status, and hunt through boxes to obtain a fresh one. Then, he'd throw the "dead" tube into a barrel beside the register. I don't know what happened to those cast-off tubes, but I do know what happened to old TVs.

My childhood stomping grounds contained ravines where farmers had disposed of rubbish for generations. This system worked when most things were made of organic materials that decomposed over time. As more things were made of metal, plastic, and glass, these piles took on greater bulk. A feather bed will decompose, but a coil-spring mattress won't. Glass canning jars can be reused, but tin cans cannot.

It was a different country then, with only half the population we now have. Young boys went about the woods and fields exploring. Junk ravines were prime spots, and we would visit them looking for bottles and tin cans to shoot.

One summer afternoon, my friends and I had been walking along a stream when we diverted uphill through the woods to investigate a rubbish ravine. I was in the lead with an air rifle when I spotted it: the holy grail of big game. It was cornered in the gully with a barbed-wire fence on two sides. It couldn't get away, and I'd seen it first. It was mine; I'd "called" it. But I didn't have the firepower to make the kill. My friends also had air rifles. What one needs to effectively bring down an old TV is a shotgun.

A bit of disagreement ensued. Our dark side emerged, and our blood lust overcame us. Jimmy aimed at the cornered TV from point-blank range and fired his air rifle. The pellet ricocheted off and flew past our heads before embedding itself in the bark of an oak tree. This close call sobered us. Still, the king of trophies was not going to defeat us, get away, or be claimed by other hunters. While Jimmy and I stood guard, Jeff ran off and returned shortly with a 20-gauge shotgun. I loaded a green shell, took aim, and blasted the cathode tube. Its vital fluids of lead, cadmium, zinc, silver, and mercury leaked out and began their journey to the water we would later drink.

The sum memory of all the TV I experienced as a youth consists of an amalgam of predictable half-hour adventures, the assassination of President Kennedy, and man landing on the moon. The rest blurs together like the memories of so many potato chips. Despite having so little to recommend it, Nancy and I introduced our young children to TV watching. If we had paid attention to the story of Jacob and Esau, we would have known better.

The book of Genesis tells the story of Isaac's sons, Jacob and Esau. Esau is the favorite of his father, a mighty hunter, and the firstborn son. Esau lives for the moment. One evening he returns home from a day of hunting. He is empty-handed, tired, and very hungry. His crafty younger brother, Jacob, the "trickster," is enjoying a steaming bowl of lentil soup. "Yum, this is great," Jacob says as he sops up his food with warm bread. "Just smell those lentils!" Jacob exclaims.

Big, hairy Esau looks down on the bubbling pot of stew. "How about it, Jacob; can I have a bowl of stew? I'm starving."

"Pull up a rock, Esau," Jacob invites as he dishes out a steaming bowl. He slathers butter on a warm chunk of bread and starts to hand it to Esau. Then he hesitates. "Esau, Dad's not going to die for years, and you get twice the inheritance I get. But Dad's rich —I stand to get a fortune too. Why don't we trade, and then you can have this bowl of lentil soup?"

Esau hesitates. His stomach growls. "What good is money later when I'm starving now?" he wonders. So he makes the trade, giving away his double portion of the estate for a bowl of soup (Genesis 25:25–34).

And so Nancy and I, tired at the end of the day, made the same deal that Esau did. Only we didn't make out quite as well as he did. All Esau lost was money. Every parent knows the rhythms of childhood. Something happens in the young brain that causes it to lose control somewhere around the time the parents are trying to get dinner on the table. A similar change takes place right before bedtime. All over the country, parents reach for help by turning on the television. We do it because it works! Prior to turning on our electronic babysitters, our children seem to demand every ounce of our attention, patience, and strength at dinnertime. On goes the set, and all our troubles melt away. Our children sit entranced, mouth breathing, gazing like reptiles at the flashing images on the screen.

When we sat Emma and Clark in front of the television, we abdicated our roles as parents. The Surgeon General and the Academy of Pediatrics recommend *no* viewing for children under two and only limited viewing for older children because of problems with obesity, sexual promiscuity, learning disorders, and attention problems. We consoled ourselves by saying that they were watching public/educational television. And perhaps it is somewhat better than commercial shows, but I'm not sure. A careful look at the public shows will reveal that there are seldom any intact families or parental role models. For the most part, TV land is politically correct, morally ambiguous, and materially oriented. God is nowhere to be found.

The main purpose of television is to sell products. I used to think that public TV was commercial free, but the branding on it is as effective, if not more so, than on commercial TV. A decade later, my kids can still rattle off the sponsors of their favorite "educational" shows.

Who are the people that control television programmers and advertisers? Most of us don't live in Hollywood or on Madison Avenue. We don't get a chance to meet our children's electronic sitter face to face. But one day I did. Mr. Van Buren was seventy-six years old, and as his much younger wife told me, "He rules Madison Avenue." My patient scowled as she told me this, but I sensed it would have gone far worse for his wife had she forgotten to let me know. His heart was racing along at an unsteady 160 beats per minute, and he was short of breath and experiencing substernal chest pain. Certain patients test the patience of the hospital staff. God sends them to check that we are all being professionals. Mr. Van Buren was one of these patients. He told the nurse about the wonderful nurses who had cared for him in his youth. When brought his meal tray, Jack Van Buren asked the kitchen worker (paid minimum wage) whether he'd dined at such and such expensive restaurant. Mr. Van Buren went on to praise various four-star restaurants at which he was welcomed as an old friend.

The crowning moments of Jack Van Buren's life were the three Cleos he was awarded. What are Cleos? He would be glad to tell you. They are the advertising equivalents of Oscar and Grammy awards. How did he win his? How had he earned *three*? As Mrs. Van Buren explained, most ad men would give their souls to have just *one* Cleo. For his first, Jack had the ingenious idea of marketing cigarettes especially to women. He caught the wave of excessive feminism and portrayed any man not in favor of women smoking as a repressive old fool. Any woman who had not taken up smoking had a long way to go. For his second Cleo, Mr. Van Buren convinced a razor company to market ladies' disposable razors. And to earn his last Cleo, he promoted a company that chemically treated home-owners' lawns. He "put them on the map," Mrs. Van Buren proudly explained.

My patient had convinced millions to start smoking, to fill landfills with single-use razors, and to spray toxic chemicals into the watersheds. We will never be able to credit Jack Van Buren with the exact number of cases of emphysema, heart attacks, and lung cancer that resulted from his cigarette campaign, nor can the exact number of cases of leukemia and solid tissue tumors caused by the "Agent Orange" chemicals sprayed over lawns ever be determined. But for his "genius," his peers honored Jack Van Buren with their highest awards.

The last time I saw Mr. Van Buren, he was in his private hospital room. His face was plethoric and red as he spoke angrily to someone on the phone. His wife jumped up and ushered me back out of the room, closing the door behind us.

In the hallway, Mrs. Van Buren explained that her husband still owned a controlling share of the ad agency. "He's never been good at delegating. Jack still likes to manage everything," she whispered as if it were a big secret. Her husband's voice rose in the background. She smiled. "His company writes more television advertisements than half the firms on Madison Avenue put together."

I quietly explained that I had bad news: The tests pointed to a malignant thyroid tumor, which in turn had set off his rapid, irregular heart rate. Mr. Van Buren would have to learn to delegate.

We walked back into Jack's room. Overhead, suspended on a bracket, a television played.

"That idiot isn't bad, you know," Jack gestured at the TV. A steroid-enhanced man with spandex tights and a ponytail hopped around talking about how much energy one could get from using his exercise equipment.

"He's turned two dollars of steel and cheap plastic into a piece of junk that he can sell for $200 to some fool who's two hundred pounds overweight. He will use it a dozen times, tops, and not send it back after thirty days because the slob will be too embarrassed to admit to himself he's got more fat than brains. Now that's the power of advertising!" Jack pointed at the television screen with his half glasses and continued, "That kid deserves every cent he gets."

Mr. Van Buren had built empires using television and advertising. Television, all television, is financed by advertising, and advertising appeals to our worldly side. It promises something we want to be, or to have, or to obtain. It offers to provide states of mind, such as joy, power, freedom, and acceptance. It promises to take away undesirable traits—boredom, obesity, loneliness, and bad breath. It convinces us of needs we don't even know we have.

Since no product can transform the powerless into the powerful, or the timid into the brave, advertisers must use their most powerful tool, and they must use it constantly. They must lie. They convince couch-potato teens that they are brave and athletic when they drink a particular brand of soda. They convince suburban women that a 2 1/2-ton SUV is their ticket to adventure and freedom. To do this, they name the gas-guzzling, polluting, expensive, hard-to-park, easily wrecked vehicle the Escape, Explorer, Trailblazer, Pathfinder, Amazon, or Yukon. They promise the spendaholic a way out of debt by taking on another loan called "debt consolidation" or "payment relief." A moment's reflection will reveal that daredevil athleticism is not enhanced by sugar water, "escapes" are not made in $30,000 gas guzzlers, and spending less —not borrowing more—is the only way out of debt.

How can Mr. Van Buren convince an intelligent woman that smoking is good for her? He must lie, repeatedly, and make her believe that she is the most important person in the world. *You* deserve a break today! *You* deserve zingy pop cereal's explosion of taste in your mouth! To obtain our diet of lies, the average American watches 1,700 hours of television annually, while the average school-age child attends only nine hundred hours of classes a year. By the time the typical person in our country reaches age seventy-one, he will have spent a solid ten waking years sitting in front of a television.

Imagine meeting God and answering the question, "What did you do with your time on earth?" You are handed a time sheet that details the seconds and decades of this precious gift called life. What will you say you have done? In a world full of trees, mountains, oceans, birds, people in need, and people to love, did you spend ten years watching the news, sitcoms, ball games, and reality shows on a cathode-ray tube? Isn't that something like wandering through the great banquet hall of life, passing by gourmet main courses and exquisite delicacies only to eat spiritual cheese puffs?

When we became Christians, Nancy and I began facing up to our dependence on the TV. We used it to ease boredom or to entertain us with a "fix" of news, excitement, or suspense, and we were teaching our children to do the same. We rationalized that we watched far less than our neighbors and rarely tuned in to commercial TV, but we knew in our hearts that television was having a negative effect on our lives. Maybe we all need an occasional escape, but do we need it 1,700 hours a year? Do we need it for even thirty minutes a day?

I had similarly rationalized much of my TV viewing while in the call room at the hospital. I was on duty, often up late at night, and it was so easy to turn it on. The TV left me with many disquieting messages: Was I getting old? Was I out of shape? Did my home look good enough? Should I replace my stereo? My computer? My car? Nothing good was happening to me while I was watching the TV. In fact, often I'd flip from channel to channel, get somewhat involved in a show, change during a commercial, and then forget the show I'd been watching.

Another doctor who occupied the call room had a better way of filling the time between patients: He would set up an easel and paint on his shifts. He said that oil paints were made for ER work because they stayed fresh for hours while he was busy seeing patients. I started avoiding the TV and instead experimented with writing, listening to lectures on tape, and reading. A calmer me walked away after the non-TV shifts. I began to keep track of my different moods and found a renewed sense of optimism when I didn't watch the tube. My wife noticed the same effect when she abstained from viewing. We weaned ourselves from the habit.

What made me determined in my resolve to stop addicting our children to television was meeting the late Jack Van Buren, King of Madison Avenue. Despite the preposterous things TV purports —such as shows about fast-moving turtles that know martial arts, or zippy actors in lab coats hired to convince kids that science and math are more fun than riding a bike down a hill—something in TV land is real. There is a real babysitter: Jack Van Buren.

The best way to teach children is to model. Nancy and I stopped watching the TV. Then we simply unplugged from the cable company. We still have the capability of watching movies at home, and even that can get out of hand. Advertising is very much a part of the film industry. There are many anti-God, anti-parent, anti-morality messages in movies, but they are more easily seen for what they are once the electronic crack habit of TV is gone.

Televisions, like their effects, are everywhere. They are now in minivans, gas stations, pubs, restaurants, shopping centers, airports, and waiting rooms. One weekend, Nancy and I were eating breakfast in a hotel's restaurant. The food was served buffet style, and many families filled the tables. At one end of the dining area, a large television was on. I looked around the room for a while, and it appeared that no one was watching the set, although during commercials many heads would turn and momentarily tune in.

I did what I frequently do now under these circumstances: I got up and turned off the TV. Within five minutes, soft conversations began to fill the dining room. I have turned off televisions in airport terminals, hospital waiting rooms, and elsewhere with similar results. Not once has anyone objected.

In C. S. Lewis's book *The Screwtape Letters*, a senior manager in hell provides advice to his nephew, who is trying to secure the soul of a man on earth. The senior manager talks lovingly of how little must be given in order to win a modern man's soul. No longer does the devil need to tempt men with extravagant sins. The vicarious experience of sin and debauchery has become enough. Why go to an island and cheat on your spouse when you can watch it on reality TV? The senior tempter especially loves noise. Heaven is a place of beautiful music, peace, and quiet. The devil wants the entire world to be filled with distracting noise.

For many, television has become more real than reality. We cry over fictitious characters and fail to respond to real friends in need. We purchase cars because of ads showing people flying along sylvan winding roads while failing to own up to a life spent in traffic. All of this has a cost to the earth and to ourselves.

Do our children sometimes tune in at a friend's house? Yes, but rarely. And not for long. My children have come to recognize television for what it is: a kind of mental junk food that is easy to get too much of. At the time we removed television from our children's world, some friends thought we might be handicapping our kids, and we even had one teacher strongly suggest that we allow regular TV viewing. Time has proven them wrong.

Cross addiction is a concept that all parents should discuss. Although every addict has his "drug of choice," cross addiction is a real and confounding problem. An alcohol addict may switch over to marijuana, and a heroin addict can live on methadone. Newer drugs and addictive substances are often safer, cheaper, and more easily obtained — or socially acceptable — than the ones they replace. Still, an addiction is an addiction. An addiction to TV can easily translate into Internet, computer gaming, or smartphone habits.

Wasting time and wasting energy are two reasons to curtail TV viewing. The three hundred million TV sets in the United States consume a lot of energy — five times more than is produced by all the geothermal, biomass, solar, and wind sources in the United States. They take energy and materials to manufacture. They are difficult to get rid of and to recycle. They convince us to buy things we don't need, which cost energy to produce, transport, and dispose of. But the real reason to worry about watching TV has to do with the part of us we can't see or measure: our spirit. Television separates us from our Creator while killing his creation.

Chapter 9

Steward Parents and Servant Children

Children do not belong to us. For a brief time, they are on loan to us from God, and we act as stewards and caretakers of them. If we have done our jobs well, in the end they will grow up and make us proud. As Christians we believe that there are more important things than happiness, wealth, and security. Although we might wish such blessings for our offspring, we are mindful that God asks us to give them faith, morality, a social conscience, and a love of all godly things. At no other time is our role of steward and our position of dominion of more importance than in childrearing.

Of necessity, we have dominion over our newborn children, but our responsibility to be stewards of what God deems sacred demands we let go of them one day. That is the real goal of all stewardship: to take a gift, nurture it, and give it away some day. Jesus is the supreme example of stewardship of a human life.

When is the right time to have a child? As every good parent knows, there is no "right" time or no "perfect" time. Because nearly everyone in America has access to birth control, we tend to overestimate our role in the timing of life's events. Having children used to be the function of simply being married, and it was a risky business. Only a few generations ago, a woman's lifetime risk of dying in childbirth was 17 percent; about one out of every five women perished this way. "With this body, I thee wed" took on profound meaning.

Children are best conceived and raised in a loving marriage. Yet in our times, children seem to pose a threat to marriage. I frequently see couples who, on the surface, appear content, but after the arrival of children their marriages fail. This is not a book about marriage or divorce — it is about the environment and stewardship — but all of these things are related. Nothing is worse for the environment than a broken family. Where once one house and one kitchen table might have sufficed, two homes, two kitchens, and two living-room sofas become a necessity.

Why do children and divorce often go together? Why was it that in times gone by, when a couple had little control over conception, birth was risky, and a child's life was tenuous, children seemed to cement families together? Why can one child exhaust two parents when our grandmothers often had six, ten, or a dozen children? Why is divorce more common as we become more affluent? Are kids more spoiled or are grown-ups? Let me define "high-maintenance children" with a story.

A number of years ago, I drove from the busy ER at a big city hospital, where I was the director, out to a rural hospital to fill in for a twenty-four-hour shift. The hospital saw a mix of blue-collar and farm workers and, because there were two nearby ski resorts, served wealthy patients as well. It had drizzled before dawn, and the temperature had dropped rapidly. Everyone was slipping and falling. In the period of a few hours, I had splinted three fractures, sewn up two faces, and repaired a huge gash on a knee.

Sewing and splinting are "bread and butter" skills for ER doctors. Of all the procedures, suturing happens to be my very favorite. I have always had an aptitude for it, and "sewing" gives me the opportunity to talk with patients and their families. I get to fix something that is broken and even see how it turns out when the patient comes back to have the sutures removed. I heard my next patient's mother before I saw her. She was two curtained cubicles away. "Just let the nurse see it, honey; he's not going to hurt you." A mother's saccharine voice rose over the curtain, repeating her plea with increasing volume.

"Okay," Sam the nurse said, "we don't have to look at it just now; we'll leave it for Dr. Sleeth to see. Let me just get your vital signs." A loud wail and sob went up. "It's okay, honey, he's just trying to take your temperature," the mother said.

I ducked out of the ER and went down to the radiology suite to look at the film of my current patient, eleven-year-old Courtney, who had fallen while walking down the stairs at her parents' farm. I flipped up the X-ray on a viewing screen, and Courtney and her father moved to stand by me. "See that?" I pointed to the area of her wrist. "That's a broken bone, which means you'll be wearing a cast for about six weeks."

After I'd splinted Courtney in the casting room, I walked back into the ER. Sam handed me a chart, saying "Your next patient fell on the slopes and cut her chin. I can't tell you how big the laceration is because she won't show it to me. She won't let me take her temperature or blood pressure either." With a deadpan look he added, "Her mother says you won't hurt her, so give me a holler if you need help."

I glanced over Debra Hill's record—age ten, no temperature, no blood pressure; allergic to amoxicillin, seafood, and any foods with bleached flour. "Hi, I'm Doctor Sleeth," I introduced myself. Debra sat on the gurney with a towel held to her chin. She was wearing a one-piece ski outfit and boots.

"Are you her mom?" I asked the woman who was similarly clad. The top of her ski suit was unzipped and folded down at the waist. She nodded. "Nice to meet you, Mrs. Hill." I shook her hand.

"It's Ms. Sender," she corrected me, and then pointed to a man and woman also sporting expensive skiwear. "These are my parents," she nodded toward them. "My husband's gone to call his parents. They're staying back at the condo."

I turned and introduced myself to my young patient. "You'll get hot in here dressed like this, Debra," I said.

"It's pronounced *De-bray*," Debra Hill's mother corrected me.

Debra glared at me as if to say, "You're not gonna see my chin, buster. I've beaten better men than you just because they brought me my sandwich with the crust on." The words of my pediatric mentor came drifting back to me. "Kids regress when they're hurt," he said, "and unfortunately so do some of their parents. If the patient is ten but acting like she's two, meet her where she is." So I took Debra off guard by saying, "Let's get you out of these boots." Little tykes will recoil if you charge in and want to look in their mouth, but they are used to depending on adults to fiddle with their shoes and socks. My mentor had taught me to always examine a scared child's feet first—because they'll let you.

Before I begin treating any child, I read them their "rights." In my book everyone has the right to the truth.

"Do you know what a lie is, Debra?" I asked. She nodded yes. "Debra, I never lie to kids. Do you understand? I never say something won't hurt if it is going to hurt. If I'm going to do anything that hurts, I will tell you." Debra's shoulders relaxed, instinctively recognizing someone telling her the truth.

It is not uncommon for someone to remove a towel from a bleeding chin and present me with a view of the mandible bone. What Debra showed me was a clean cut of less than two centimeters, running in the natural fold line under the chin. Half of the planet walks around with a small scar in the same place, the front bumper of the face.

"Oh, just a tiny cut," I soothed. "It will take only a stitch or two to fix." Debra nodded her head "okay" as I explained what was entailed.

"Can you use butterfly bandages?" Mom interrupted.

"Well, yes, it's small enough that we could get away with them."

"Which one will leave a scar?"

"All cuts heal by scarring. There will be a tiny scar no matter what is done. But usually a suture leaves less of a scar," I answered.

"But I thought you said we could use a butterfly," Mom countered. This went around a bit, and then maternal grandmother stepped forward. She glanced around the immaculate little ER as if it were a condemned chicken coop.

"I don't mean to insult you, Doctor, but shouldn't we get a second opinion? Wouldn't this case be handled better at Big City Hospital?" So off to Big City Hospital they went to have two sutures placed.

Lesson number one in steward parenting: The prince of the world has already come. His bassinet was a feed trough in a barn. The Lord of Lords, the Prince of Peace, the Messiah made it into this world without the use of multiple sonograms. His parents did not interview dozens of midwives, obstetricians, birth coaches, and birthing centers.

The most important parenting step we can take is to grow up ourselves and recognize that the world does not need another prince or princess. It needs servants of justice, truth, compassion, and love—in short, it needs servants of God. If the parents do not serve God, they will end up being the servants of their children, and this leads to situations like the three generations of De-bra.

Although those types of parents constantly relate how much they love their children, and how they are willing to do anything for them, they often end up resenting the very monsters they have created.

By pure accident, Nancy and I got some of our early parenting right, but we got a lot wrong, too. Mostly, we were too selfish ourselves because we did not serve God. When we finally found that there was a universe beyond our wants and desires, we began to parent off the same page. This brings up another principle of parenting: Raise a child with too much love and not enough discipline, as we initially did, and it can be straightened out in a few months. Raise a child with too much discipline and not enough love, and it takes a lifetime to correct. Balance is the byword of good parenting.

Dr. Luden, a psychiatrist friend of mine, frequently offers this advice: He holds out his left hand and says, "Some parents are way out here with children. They're very nurturing, laid back, and encouraging." Then he holds out his right hand and says, "Some parents are way out here—you know, floss your teeth every night, make your bed perfectly every morning. I never see the kids from either one of these kinds of families." Then he stretches both hands wide apart. "I make my living by taking care of kids who have one parent at each end of the spectrum, the kind of parents who are working off very different pages. The really messed-up kids have parents who are inconsistent, have shifting rules and boundaries, and are at odds with one another."

With Dr. Luden's advice in mind, consider the following scenario: You walk into a room and one of the kids is screaming. Earlier the same day, they were fighting and you gave them a time-out. Now you say, "To your rooms for a *double* time-out!"

Your spouse was present when you were out of the room and

realizes that you got the situation wrong and that Suzy was screaming because she hurt herself and Billy had nothing to do with it. If your spouse raises her voice and begins to argue with you in front of the children, then your marriage and your parenting are in trouble. This is not a misprint. Your spouse should support you (and vice versa) even in your minor mistakes. It is more important for a child to know that his parents are supportive of each other and working off the same page than to see them at odds.

Any child will instantly forgive you if a few moments later you walk into his room and say, "Your mom and I talked things over, and I didn't realize that you hit your own head and you and your brother weren't fighting. I'm sorry." Apologize to anyone — especially your spouse and children if you are wrong — but always parent together; do it reflexively and instinctively.

I frequently encountered families in the ER with one or two children whose minor cold symptoms have thrown them into near desperate straits of exhaustion. One spoiled child can wear down two parents, three day-care workers, and four grandparents. On dozens of occasions, I have heard a parent lament and wonder, "I don't know how my grandmother did it. She raised seven kids after her husband died, without any help, and they all went to college." Grandma did it without an au pair, television, windup rocker, or microwave oven. She did it because she was better at it.

When Nancy and I learned to say, "Go to your rooms for a time-out, Clark and Emma," instead of trying to adjudicate their childish disagreements, harmony began to reign between them and us.

How are saving energy, buying less, and recycling more powerful adjuncts to spiritual parenting? Because earth stewardship is about giving, not taking. Judging by Debra's behavior, I'd bet the farm that she never had been given a job, like tearing labels off tin cans before putting the paper and can in their separate recycling bins. Jesus says that the truest kind of giving is when the recipient cannot repay you. Recycling is a gift of hope.

An integral part of giving is not taking. This is seen in any situation in which resources are limited. If ten people have only one loaf of bread between them, it becomes clear that the first tenant of sharing is not eating more than one-tenth of a loaf.

Another adjunct of giving comes from learning to think abstractly. By this I mean that one must come to feel the needs, pain, and suffering of others as if they were personal experiences. When we teach our children the joy of giving, they must learn it on the physical, mental, and spiritual planes. When we assign tasks such as weeding the garden, hanging clothing on the line, or hand-washing dishes, we assign a physical task, but the motivations of the physical act are abstracts that must be learned. We teach our children to recycle paper, to take out the compost, and to turn out the lights without reminders when they come to understand that what they are doing has a direct benefit for a poor child in Senegal or Indonesia. The spiritual lesson they learn is compassion.

Every church, school, and library ought to own a copy of the book *Material World: A Global Family Portrait*. This book provides a physical representation of how blessed we are materially in the United States and how much poverty abounds in our world. I've always found it interesting that missionaries' children who live in physically impoverished countries throughout the world rarely complain about hardships, and that many even follow in their parents' footsteps. Clark and Emma understand that they are doing third-world mission work by sending these countries cleaner air and water, as well as financial donations.

Perhaps most important, we need to teach our children to give on a spiritual level. When children pray with adults, they need to hear prayers that extend beyond selfish and parochial wants. They need to hear us pray on behalf of those in poverty, ignorance, and pain. Our prayers must mirror God's concerns, from the smallest sparrow to the most needy prisoner.

I am compelled to discuss competitive sports, an obsession of our society, because they are closely linked with childrearing. Ours is not the first age to worship athletes and games, but it surprises many to learn we are the first in modern times. Not since the time of imperial Rome has the world been so taken with competitive games. When civilization retired the pagan gods Zeus, Athena, and Nike, they retired the Olympic Games. No stadium of any size was constructed on the planet for over fifteen hundred years afterward. Humanity turned its building skills to churches, hospitals, and colleges. Then, in 1896, the Olympics were reborn. Thirty years later, they came into their own when Adolph Hitler hosted and promoted the 1936 Olympic Games.

For people who worshipped materialism above all, Rome put on the show. "Give them bread and circus" (circus being a stadium for games), Rome's politicians declared, "and we can rule the world." The payoff for Romans taking over your city was to have them build a stadium.

Yet Jesus is silent on the subject of sports. None of the gospels mention sports. And Paul mentions athletic training only as a metaphor for spiritual fitness. Why? Is it because getting into heaven has nothing to do with being a sports fan? Could it be that the victor/vanquished model inherent in sports has no analog in God's kingdom? Is it because sports are a glorification of temporal man, and not of God? Is it because if we simply believe in Jesus, we win?

Physical activity is necessary to a wholesome life. But a growing state-sponsored and state-promoted worship of sports is in con-

STEWARD PARENTS AND SERVANT CHILDREN

flict with church and family. When sports compete with God in America, God loses.

I attend a "Bible-believing" church, but members sometimes miss worship services to transport children to sports events. We tell our children that we believe in Jesus, but do we tacitly wink when we opt for a childhood devoted to sports? Do we really mean, "It's not whether you win or lose, but how you play the game," when we also say, "No one ever won the silver; they lost the gold"?

I once attended a football game as the official physician. It looked to me like the home team and its coach played ethically. The opposing coach had his team get on their knees and pray for victory. This coach broke the first three of the Ten Commandments in the first thirty seconds of the game. His language was abhorrent, but his behavior was worse. The screaming fans were unaware, and when he was presented with a trophy at the conclusion of the game, the head of the school thanked God that they were "blessed" with the "coach's winning gifts." Jesus tells us not to judge, but surely what I saw was blasphemous.

The modern style of highly competitive sports takes away from children the chance to play. They no longer have much time for pickup games of baseball or kickball; if they're not practicing for the next big game, they're traveling hours to attend it. Teenagers often sustain injuries that require reconstruction of their knees and other joints. As resources become more scarce, we will have to decide whether we should use millions of gallons of fuel transporting teens to games they will never play as adults, or whether we should instead consider those around the globe who do not have enough fuel to cook dinner. Will we spend millions on uniforms to be worn for a season, or will we do as Christ instructs and clothe the poor?

As the Bible clearly states, "No man can serve two masters."

It is up to parents to help children choose wisely whom they will serve. The good news is that by following the words of Jesus, everyone can be a winner.

In talking about sports, and earlier about television, I have really been focusing on the "don'ts" of modern parenting, not the "dos." The dos are so numerous as to be unlistable. Others frequently tell me how wonderful my children are, and how lucky I am to have them. Often this is a result of them doing some kind of selfless act for others. I cannot thank God enough for the thousands of hours we have spent together reading out loud, listening to music, hiking, and lying out at night and viewing the stars. But the time is approaching when Nancy and I must give them away.

I brag here only to lend some credibility to the advice I give younger parents. When Emma was eleven, she and I were home alone when a friend of mine dropped by to unload his troubles. I asked Emma to excuse us, and my friend and I went to a separate room to talk. An hour later, Emma knocked on the door. In she breezed with an elaborate "snack" featuring a homemade soufflé. Back and forth she ran to the kitchen until a meal, silverware, and drinks were laid before our guest. Then off Emma went. My friend felt so blessed by Emma's gesture that he was literally in tears.

Similarly, when my son was in high school, Clark was visiting a friend when a big storm blew past. A large tree fell across an elderly neighbor's driveway. My son and his friend spent the next five hours sawing up the tree. When they were done, the elderly couple offered the boys money, which they refused. I learned of their work only when I received a letter from the couple, introducing themselves and relating their gratitude.

Last week, I put Emma on a plane to visit her brother at college, where she also plans to study. As Emma passed through the airport gate, I could no longer accompany her. I watched as she took off her shoes for the metal detector. What a strange and scary world it is, I thought. In stocking feet, she appeared small and vulnerable. She smiled back at me, clearly nervous, and then blew me a kiss. The first thing she picked up from the X-ray conveyor belt was her worn Bible, held together with duct tape. I silently asked God to look over her. A feeling of peace came over me. For a moment I pictured her in chain mail, protected by the armor of God.

We cannot keep our children from the future. Civilization's next chapter looks uncertain, full of change and darkness. What is our job as steward parents? We can do everything in our power to be a light that shines into the unknown, and we can send our children forward dressed in the full armor of God: Equip them with the belt of truth, the breast plate of righteousness, the helmet of salvation, the shield of faith, and the sword of God that we love one another (Ephesians 6:14–17). Do these things and not only will the world enjoy their company now, but you will get to enjoy the company of your children in heaven for eternity.

Chapter 10

Food for Thought

I once heard a description of what meals are like in heaven. The saints are seated on either side of a four-foot-wide banquet table. The table is set with delicious foods on every plate. The only thing that appears out of the ordinary is the silverware. All the utensils have three-foot-long handles. The dinnertime rule is that everyone must eat using the long forks and spoons. Amazingly, the dining room in hell is designed exactly the same. What makes heaven heavenly and hell hellish? In heaven, the diners immediately set about feeding their brothers and sisters across the table using the perfectly proportioned utensils, while in hell each person rages at the ill-fitting utensils as they attempt the impossible task of feeding themselves.

Our relationships to what we eat and to each other are important here on earth. We humans have the ability to eat a highly varied diet. We can eat fungi, mollusks, birds, grains, fermented foods, nuts, insects, flowers, tree sap, bees' honey, fish eggs, cow's milk, and plant roots. It is a wonder and a marvel. Who figured out that the bark on one tree made cinnamon and the bark of another made poison? We will never know. Our relationship to food is vital. Food is not an option. It is a necessity. We can merely eat our fill, or we can be nourished. We can choose foods that are good for us or ones that do us long-term harm. Our choice of diets can encourage sustainable, ethical farming, or we can support agriculture that is out of sync with long-term planetary and human health.

In the framework of Christian tradition, no food is inherently bad. On the contrary, Christianity is unique in its lack of dietary restrictions. Christ instructs us not to worry about what we eat (Matthew 6:25). He says that nothing we ingest defiles us; rather, it is the words that come out of us that betray our evil hearts. In Acts, chapter 10, God commands Peter to eat any and all foods. From that day forward, kosher restrictions no longer limited the fellowship of the followers of Christ.

Yet because Christianity has so few restrictions on what we eat, what we wear, when we marry, et cetera, we are called to bring a moral and ethical view to every aspect of life. This is the meaning of Christ telling us to be as perfect as God in heaven (Matthew 5:46–48). Although Christianity carries no specific injunctions about eating, Christian morality does. The first such moral injunction arises during a food shortage. There is no specific commandment that says, "Thou shall not eat all you want." However, the Christian morality is clear: We are to put the needs of others before us, up to and including laying down our life for another. We are to look after the weak, meek, and hungry. In a situation of food shortage, we should eat no more than a "fair share."

A second reason to abstain from a food is if it was obtained through an immoral means—for instance, food that is stolen or gotten by child or slave labor. Additionally, God intends us to treat animals with respect. So food that is obtained from mistreated or tortured animals should be avoided.

A third consideration is the consumption of food directly harmful to us. The Bible instructs us to care for our bodies as if they were temples of God (1 Corinthians 6:19). That's part of the rationale behind avoiding gluttony and drunkenness.

Lastly, our morals exclude us from eating food if the growing, harvesting, storing, or cooking of it is harmful to others. This falls under the umbrella of the Golden Rule (Matthew 7:12).

So at least four moral considerations exist that can call us to alter our diet. The first is a food shortage; the second is to avoid food obtained by unethical means; the third is to avoid food harmful to us; and the last is to abstain from food that causes harm to others.

These are the considerations that compel me to write about food, though I have a natural reluctance to do so. In our affluent society, it seems that narcissism and food obsessions travel hand in hand. Often, those on either end of the scale — people who insist on organic free-range broccoli and people who salivate over pan-fried baby dolphin — care about nothing but themselves. The last thing the world needs is more people obsessed by what they eat. A second reason I am reluctant to write about food is because the subject is tied to body weight. In my experience, there is no connection between the size of someone's waist and their heart.

Still, the Bible demands that we treat our bodies with respect. We are not to wantonly abuse them. That is why the average person should eat a moderate, reasonably balanced diet. Maintaining a body weight within 20 percent of what is ideal and eating a diet along the lines of the nutritionists' food pyramid (a foundation of grains, with a small amount of fats and sweets at the apex) seems prudent. However, many today eat a diet that resembles the food obelisk.

In our home, we eat meals together. This means what it says: We sit down at the same time and eat the food that is offered without picking or complaining.

Eating together and sharing the same food is integral to the story of Christ. One of his most spectacular miracles was performed before a crowd of five thousand (Matthew 14:15). Jesus took five loaves of bread and two fish and blessed them. From this, his disciples fed the multitudes. Now imagine if Jesus was faced with a group of typical modern Americans. Many would not sacrifice a meal to hear his words. Others might say, "Kids don't eat fish. Do you have any hot dogs?" Or "Yuck! I don't eat fish with the head on. Can you take it back and remove the head?" Or "Is this pumpernickel bread? I don't like pumpernickel." Any eating habit that draws us inward and away from a grateful relationship with God and each other is, well, sinful.

Is eating meat a sin? Many environmentalists say that we should avoid meat or change the amount and type of meat we eat. I used to take these calls for vegetarianism as just radical New Age philosophy. But after studying the issue, I have changed my mind. Ten times more energy, water, and grain is needed to produce a pound of beef or pork than to produce a pound of milk or cheese. The four moral reasons for changing our diet all come into play when considering beef and pork. Let me discuss the change in how animals used to be treated and the new circumstances many live in now.

As children, my siblings and I played in the barn. We took eggs from beneath hens that roosted in individual boxes lined with straw. We climbed on the chicken-house roof and under its raised floor. We milked Holstein cows that grazed outside and nursed their own offspring. These are no longer the conditions under which our current supply of meat and dairy products are produced.

I recently toured a "cage-free, organic" chicken farm. I was shown into the egg processing room, where four thousand eggs are sorted and washed each hour. The noise was deafening, and workers shouted their greetings as I was introduced. "Do you want to see one of the barns?" my guide yelled.

"Sure," I hollered back. We went down an enclosed corridor as hundreds of eggs went in the opposite direction on a conveyor belt. Then we entered one of the farm's six cage-free barns. It contained fourteen thousand chickens. They fed from pneumatic chutes, drank from hydraulic nozzles, and defecated on the floor. "What's that?" I yelled, pointing toward an electrical device in a corner. My guide cupped his hands beside my ear and, yelling, explained that it delivers a shock to keep chicks out of the corners. As I mentioned, old-fashioned chicken coops provide each of the hens with a straw-lined box to roost in. Without such a nest, a bird is driven to seek out a "safe" corner in which to rest. In a barn with fourteen thousand chickens and only four corners, the birds suffocate themselves trying to roost together. My guide said that one of the shock devices had malfunctioned a few weeks before and nearly a thousand of the chickens had died. They used snow shovels and wheelbarrows to remove the corpses.

The barn that I toured housed "mature" chickens. In the short time they had been alive, they had never seen the light of day, felt the wind, or had a moment's rest or security. Most had lost a substantial portion of their feathers. After nine months on earth, this particular batch had a date two days hence with a soup factory. A chicken is not the most appealing of God's creatures. It doesn't have big eyes; it's not naturally affectionate or intelligent. It doesn't have a melodious voice. Yet I was deeply disturbed by this scene. The noise and the overpowering ammonia-like smell were only part of my distress. Everything that God represents—peace, quiet, and dignity—was missing. My grandparents would have called this factory barn the work of the devil.

Two thousand years ago, Christ was born in a barn and laid in a feed box. This was a humble beginning, but not a cruel or unsafe one. In contrast, no one on the planet would want to give birth to a child in a modern factory barn. There are many industrial farms in our land in which animals never see a star, feel the warmth of the sun, or enjoy the rain. They live unable to lie down, suckle from their mothers, or mate. Animals that God created as vegetarians, such as cows, are fed other cows that have been industrially processed. In order to survive, they are given antibiotics and supplements. Dairy cows are injected with hormones that cause their udders to swell and produce more milk.

Surely if the God in heaven is the author of our Bible, he is displeased with the treatment of animals in industrial farms. To excuse this sort of mistreatment, some quote the "dominion" phrase out of context. They ignore the Bible's hundreds of guidelines about the ethical treatment of animals. How far does God's reverence for animal life go? Consider Exodus 23:5 (NLT): "If you see the donkey of someone who hates you struggling beneath a heavy load, do not walk by. Instead, stop and offer to help." Recall also that God's concern for livestock is carved in the Ten Commandments (Exodus 23:12 and the fourth commandment). Jesus is the "Good Shepherd." I cannot believe that a good shepherd would keep animals that normally lie down to sleep standing in cages their entire lives, nor would he leave lights on twenty-four hours a day with the sounds of machinery and animals in pain ringing in their ears.

Our current food supply is largely a product of the consumer movement that grew in the 1960s and 1970s. It started for good reasons, and with the best of intentions. But when consumerism becomes the driving ethic, it has only one commandment: Get the most by paying the least. In this system, dignity, ethics, beauty, fairness, and families that live on small farms do not figure. The only line is the bottom line.

When a family decides to change its diet to support ethical farming, it must make a decision to spend a little more and look a little harder. It will have to eat less of some foods and more of others. Eating less beef and pork is a great way to start. I name these two because their total impact on the planet is the greatest.

To obtain billions of hamburger patties for a few cents each, America's fast-food restaurants buy much of their meat from Central and South American farmers. These farmers clear-cut forests, often starting a cattle-raising process that can be sustained for only a few short years. The loss of rain forests in South America means that the clouds they once made no longer blow across the Atlantic to drop their water on Africa. As a result, the Sahara grows by thousands of acres a year. What is the bottom line for Africans? More starvation. And the bottom line for Americans? Cheap burgers and growing waistlines.

The Heifer Project, a hunger relief organization, says that nearly a billion people live in chronic hunger. Every ten days, a quarter of a million people starve to death — that's twenty-five thousand per day. Caring for these people is not an optional activity for the followers of Christ.

To fight world hunger, we need to do more than send money to relief organizations, although that is a vital part. We need to change the manner in which we eat. My mother used to tell us to eat everything on our plate. "There are starving kids in India," she would say. I couldn't figure out the connection as a child, but it appears she was ahead of her time. It does matter to children around the world what we put on our plates.

I have struggled to cut down on the meat and calories I eat. It has been a long process, and I'm making headway. I have never worried about my waistline or health, but, finally, I have a motivation for change. It's those starving kids in India, Africa, and Central America. Our family simply does not eat at fast-food places. We have gradually dropped meat, first from breakfast, then from lunch, and now from several dinners weekly. There are many other foods we have simply given up.

Cutting down on certain foods is good for our health and the planet, while caring about where our food comes from and what conditions it and its growers live under is good for the soul.

Nancy and I were working in our garden late this summer. It was a perfect day, a day that defies the rules of grammar—it was "more perfect" than all the days before it. We were putting some parts of the garden to rest, while in another section we harvested carrots and potatoes. Late in the day we sat together to weed the strawberry patch. A feeling of joy and peace overcame me. I felt close to God. I experienced "the peace that passes all understanding." I was in communion with the saints and with Nancy. Do you know why?

God created a man and a woman to work together in a garden. We were doing what our Maker designed us to do, and we were reaping the spiritual blessings. Each year our garden grows in square footage and in feeding capacity. We compost all our table scraps, and they complete a cycle by becoming fertilizer. We use no chemicals, and we rotate crops annually. In the garden's seventh year, we will let it sit fallow, as the Bible instructs.

We have begun canning large amounts of garden produce using a pressure cooker. This means we have a pantry filled with aesthetic jars that require no refrigeration. When unexpected visitors arrive for dinner (which occurs so frequently that it cannot be called unexpected), we do not need to dash off to a grocery store.

Of all the areas ripe for ministry and missions, gardening is at the top. Around the country, churches are finding this to be true. An abandoned lot in the inner city is the perfect place to start a youth ministry. All of the principles of God's love and sustaining care for us can be illustrated. Reverend Dale White, a retired

Methodist minister and bishop, practices garden evangelism. On one project he had little funding. He brought his inner-city children with him as he visited hardware and garden stores asking for donations. He has a photograph of a dozen of them staring up over a store counter. "What person can resist giving them a shovel, seeds, or a chance?" he asks. The children see something besides a government handout. They see Christian charity. As Christ says, "By this all people will know you."

No church can expect to win a single soul by maintaining mowed grass lawns. But this is not true if those grounds are tilled up and made into community gardens. What better place to share the Good News about living water, the Good Shepherd, or the tree that bears fruit than in a church garden or orchard?

Another downside of our modern dependency on processed foods is that it keeps neighbors from useful interactions. It prevents Christians from having points of contact with nonbelievers. It is my hope that not only will the church provide the moral leadership necessary to make earth stewardship a reality, but that it will become a means of evangelizing to this next generation, who is acutely aware of impending environmental problems.

The gardening ministries of Bishop White and many others work because the point of contact between humanity, God, and nature is a biblical one. The Bible says that God formed man out of the soil of the garden. Jesus presents his metaphors of heaven in terms of nature. The kingdom of heaven, he tells us, is a seed that grows into a mighty tree. It is the yeast that causes the flour to rise. It is a school of fish caught in a net. Christ does not use metaphors peculiar to his day. He does not say that the kingdom is like a chariot race or a richly woven fabric or even a beautiful temple. No, the kingdom is like a grapevine. God makes the waters flow, part, and become walkable. He is the master of all nature.

Diamonds, gold, and jewelry were more popular in Jesus's day than even now. They were portable wealth in a time before banks. I do not think it was by chance that the only jewel he mentions is the pearl. What separates the pearl from all other gemstones? It is the only one that is made by life: the oyster. Where there is life, there is God, and where there is God, there is life. From the beginning to the end of the Bible, God demands a reverence for life.

Many of the churches I visit enjoy a coffee hour after service. It's a wonderful tradition. I'm glad that many congregations are recognizing the moral implications of their coffee hour by switching to shade-grown, or fair-trade, coffee.

Having practiced medicine in the mountains of Central America, I can assure any church or individual that the decision to switch from clear-cut, fungicide- and fertilizer-dependent coffee to shade-grown coffee has a dramatically favorable impact on the lives of families in the third world. The water downstream from clear-cut coffee plantations is undrinkable. Conversely, shade-grown coffee is good for the soil. It allows workers to labor in the shade rather than the blazing sun. And as with almost all ethically grown produce, it tastes better.

Hundreds of food-related decisions can benefit others or ultimately cause harm. A full discussion of this topic is beyond the scope of this book, but first steps are surprisingly easy — and satisfying — to take. Find ways of buying, cooking, and storing food that use less energy. Pick an area like gardening, or buying locally raised produce, or cutting down on meat and searching out local sources, and begin.

My grandmother used to say, "You are what you eat." She was a gardener and a canner. Her garden provided a substantial number of the calories her children ate. If her saying is true, then I worry about many children today. They are an amalgam of genetically altered, fertilized, chemically sprayed, force-fed, hormone-driven tissue raised by inhumane means. I wonder whether this contributes to why many walk around with a sense of gnawing spiritual hunger—even though they eat too many calories. It is something to think about. It's food for thought.

Chapter 11

A House Is Not a Home

One Friday afternoon last February, I found myself struggling up a dirt trail in the mountains of Central America. The path was so steep that I had difficulty breathing, and I often needed to grab onto a clump of vegetation to steady myself. I followed Tina, who was taking a few weeks from her Peace Corps job to help our small medical mission team negotiate this mountainous terrain. My daughter and three other teens followed us, laden with backpacks of medicine.

We turned off the trail and headed straight up a rocky path that led to the home of the village spokesperson. His hut was surprisingly well constructed for the area, with two rooms built of homemade brick. I was introduced, then taken out to the porch to begin a clinic. A number of families queued up, arranged from oldest to youngest.

I had been taking care of patients for a few hours when a woman in her thirties sat down. Her ear had been bothering her for the last three days, and she was unable to sleep at night. I took a quick look and realized that I needed to irrigate her ear canal, so I rigged up a syringe and needle and set to work. When I flooded her ear with water, out came a live spider the size of my thumbnail. It began crawling on her blouse. I picked up the spider and placed it in the bushes. It was the kind of case I love: One minute the patient is in too much discomfort to sleep; the next, she is cured.

We saw patients and handed out medicines until our backpacks were empty, and then the village leader asked if I would visit an ill woman who could not get out of bed. I led the group back around the house and started down the mountain.

"No, no, Doctor," our host shouted in Spanish. "She is up this way." So we began a twenty-minute climb straight up the mountain. The entire village decided to come along. Children literally ran circles around us as the "gringo" teens and I struggled up in the blazing sun.

"Welcome," a small woman greeted us. "Thank you for coming to see my mother." I ducked low to make it under the doorway. Their home was one room with the corner partially portioned off with sticks. The hut had no windows, and the light from the front door was being blocked by the dozens of children and adults peering in. A flame smoldered in the mud fireplace in the far corner. There was no chimney; the smoke that made it out of the house wafted out through the open eaves.

I dug in my pack, pulled out my stethoscope and a flashlight, and stepped around the stick "wall." There on a bed lay Marta-Mary. No one was certain of Marta-Mary's age, but I guessed she had made it into her late fifties or maybe early sixties.

When I say that Marta-Mary lay on a bed, I take a liberty. Her "bed" was a pallet of sticks covered with straw and a few rags.

"Can you talk?" I asked. Tina repeated my question in Spanish. No answer. "Can you hear me?" A slight nod. She lay in a crumpled ball, her back to me. She gazed in an unfocused malaise at the hole in the crumbling mud-and-daub wall. "I'm going to move you so I can look at you," I said, and I put my arms under her and lifted her onto her back. I gently pulled back a torn blanket. I smelled, and then saw, her bowels—they were exposed by a cancer that had eaten away her abdominal wall. How had she made it this long?

"What is it, Daddy?" Emma whispered. I had not realized that my fourteen-year-old daughter was at my shoulder.

"It's an untreated cancer," I replied.

"Can you do something?"

"No, not about the cancer," I said.

I asked the woman if it hurt. Yes, it did. I dug in my pack and pulled out a precious bottle of morphine tablets. Someone back in the States had donated the unused portion of his prescription to our cause. Now was the time to give the pills away. Tina set about the task of translating how to use them, then put the pills in a bag along with pictures showing how much and how often to use the medicine.

I explained the obvious to Marta-Mary's daughter. "Your mother is going to die very soon. There is nothing I can do other than help with her pain." The daughter thanked me, and I learned that Marta-Mary was much beloved by the neighbors. She had always been generous. I glanced around the hut. It had no windows, no water, no electricity, no closets, no chimney, no chest of drawers. It had a few grain sacks and some hanging dried plants. A picture of Jesus, cut from a magazine, was tacked to the wall.

I came out into the hot sun and was motioned by the crowd to an area under a tree. I was offered a chair to use and was surprised to see that it was a battered, old hospital commode. Sitting on a hospital commode—even a clean, gleaming one—is not something doctors do in public back home.

I began to say that I'd rather stand. Then I realized that the chair had not been there when we first came. Someone must have pulled it from his home; the commode was perhaps the only chair in the village, a seat of honor.

A deep flush of shame came over me, which has lasted until this day. The entire village was offering the best that they had, and it wasn't good enough for me. I sat down. God humbles the proud.

Schoolchildren memorize that "food, clothing, and shelter" are the necessities of life. Who provides these necessities, our "daily bread"? God. But we must know God to acknowledge his gifts. As we wake up to our distance from God, we begin the process of changing our lives. The natural consequence of knowing God is to want to know him more.

Even devout Christians can have doubts. "Am I really saved? Am I really going to heaven?" I am not a theologian, and yet I believe that our salvation is a gift we don't deserve. It must be anticipated on the basis of faith, as there is nothing we can do to earn it. Yet faith without works can be a sign that salvation is not ours.

Chapter 18 in the Gospel of Luke describes a young man approaching Jesus. The man asks what he must do to make it into heaven. Jesus says that he must follow the Ten Commandments. The man replies:

> "I've obeyed all these commandments since I was a child."
>
> "There is one more you lack," Jesus said. "Sell all you have and give the money to the poor, and you will have treasure in heaven. Then come, follow me." But when the man heard this, he became sad because he was very rich.
>
> Jesus watched him go and then said to his disciples, "How hard it is for rich people to get into the Kingdom of God! It is easier for a camel to go through the eye of

a needle than for a rich person to enter the Kingdom of God!" (Luke 18:21–25 NLT)

It is not our possessions or our homes that will keep us out of heaven, but our *unwillingness* to set them aside in service of the Lord.

Over the past five years, our home has ceased to be "our" home and has turned instead into a center for mission and ministry. This was not an overnight process but an ongoing and continually evolving one. Our eventual goal is for "our" house to become the Lord's.

The first movement in our home was toward mission, or helping those around the world in need. People look up to missionaries. They hold a special status, and they deserve it, as well as our prayers and financial support. However, we cannot all be missionaries physically serving in third-world countries. But we can begin to open our minds, hearts, and homes to worldwide mission work. The first mission work we did to help the poor in other countries was to recycle religiously and to stop buying any products made out of rain-forest timber.

How does refraining from buying a teak chair for your deck constitute mission work? Remember Marta-Mary's home? In order to get to it, I must fly into a coastal city. Compared to that city, Marta-Mary's home is a haven of safety and dignity. Nonetheless, tides of rural farmers in Central America, South America, Africa, and Asia are forced to abandon lands they have worked for generations and flood the cities. They flee the mountains because their homes are being destroyed. As the demand for deck chairs, plywood underlayment, disposable chopsticks, and teak furniture grows, the trees in the third world are cut down. Poor families often do not own the land they have worked. They have no say and make no profit from the cutting of trees. Yet cutting down the forests around them changes their world. The topsoil washes away. The streams dry up. The trees God planted to hold the land in place are gone, so when a hurricane comes, the hillsides simply collapse and wash away.

The cities of poor countries contain small enclaves of enormous wealth and huge populations of frightened, huddled masses. Childhood prostitution, gangs, violence, and corruption are the norm. The city I traveled through to reach Marta-Mary has guards armed with AK−47s patrolling every gas station, bank, and hotel—any place where people have money or food. I used to ask myself, "Why would families leave a farm—no matter how poor—to live in a cardboard box outside of São Paulo, Brazil; Lagos, Nigeria; or Calcutta, India?" The answer: Their farms have become unlivable, often owing to the outside influences of the global economy.

Haiti's forests have been cut down and shipped to developed nations. As a result, Haiti has lost 90 percent of its topsoil, which in turn has contributed to the ingrained poverty of the country and exacerbated the effects of natural disasters. And it is precisely these displaced families who are least able to escape the ravages of a climate gone ill.

So our family's first home mission was to try to keep a third-world farm family on their land. Recycling an aluminum can helps prevent an African mountain from being leveled by dynamite and earthmovers. Not using throwaway chopsticks can keep an eight-year-old out of a brothel in Indonesia. God calls us to get involved in every aspect of saving humanity. It's what Jesus gave his life for.

In addition to making our house a mission base to the world, we are cleaning up our own backyard. Nothing is so aptly named as junk mail. The paper from these mountains of un-asked-for mail comes from trees, and the dyes come from chemicals around the world. Four out of every five pieces of junk mail are not recycled. Junk mail fills 340,000 garbage trucks a year, all bound for landfills, and the dioxin created in the papermaking process means that I can't eat a fish out of the Androscoggin River without risking cancer. Charity and recycling begin at home.

In my first year of medical school, I took a course called Embryology, from which, only years afterward, I learned a lesson about earth care. Embryology is the study of how humans develop from an egg and sperm into a kicking, crying, cooing individual. The process is a marvel and a miracle. From the nanosecond the egg and sperm come together, a complicated ballet of atoms, amino acids, and proteins starts. In that moment, the egg completely changes and becomes impervious to any other hopeful sperm. We tend to think of things slowing down as a baby approaches birth, but in the moments surrounding birth, a final symphony of change occurs. The circulation of the body instantaneously reverses and abandons the umbilical flow. Lungs that have never been exposed to air must expand for the first time.

The one thing that newborn babies don't have to learn to do is to swallow. They've been practicing the swallowing reflex for months. What do they drink in the womb? Amniotic fluid. Why do they drink? Because they are thirsty. Their bodies are losing fluid. "How?" you ask. They can't sweat, but their kidneys are making urine. The urine fills the bladder, and as most everyone knows, a baby's bladder simply empties itself when it is full. Baby urine is one of the main ingredients of amniotic fluid.

Thank goodness we're designed so we forget what we drank in the womb. As a young doctor, however, I got a reminder. I was in the second year of residency, covering the OB ward, when I was called to deliver a baby. Once in a while, as in this case, the mother's water does not break before the baby decides to make an appearance. This particular woman was in the final stages of labor with her amniotic sac still intact. It bulged out like a tense water balloon. I was turning to pick up a towel off the stand when the "balloon" exploded. The force of the explosion knocked off my glasses, and a quart of ninety-nine-degree amniotic fluid shot up my nose, behind my mask, and down my gaping mouth. I was temporarily blinded, and I couldn't spit out the fluid because of the soaked mask. I was sputtering and sightless, and the baby was coming!

Praise the Lord for nurses. One of them tore off the mask and began mopping my face. Another recovered my glasses and got them back on me. I managed to catch the baby, but not before swallowing a mouthful of "fluid."

Babies and mothers recover quickly from such incidents, but it took me years to really understand the lesson I was being taught that day: God designs intricate closed-loop systems. Anything we throw away we will eat, or drink, or breathe again. Our mother's womb is a sort of microcosmos that reflects the larger world.

The quickest measure of a household's waste is how much trash it makes. As a family, we committed ourselves to reducing that amount by about four-fifths. We've achieved that goal, and I hope someday we go to zero.

Along the way, Nancy began a small vegetable garden. I wasn't much help in it for years, but now we till, plant, weed, and harvest together. She needed rich soil, so we started composting all our table scraps. We stopped using a garbage disposal, and we no longer throw organic matter in the trash.

We also began "precycling." Now we think about how much trash, waste, or packaging a product will produce before we buy it. This often leads us toward buying in bulk, which is less expensive and entails fewer trips to stores. Our "best buys" are simply to forgo a purchase altogether. If the product is cheaply made and might easily break, it represents another kind of waste. We balance quality with overall cost and the amount of packaging that comes with a product.

In general, we've come to realize that if we've lived without it for the first twenty-five years of our marriage, we can probably do without it forever. If we've made it this long slicing vegetables by hand, there is no point in adding a "slice-o-matic" to our lives. Unless an item is broken and cannot be repaired, we will not replace it just because it is out of fashion.

To cut down on trash and recycling, we also cancelled our newspaper and magazine subscriptions. If I really want to know something about current events, I borrow the neighbor's newspaper or read one at the library. Speaking of which—book buying has always been a weakness of ours. Now we try to limit book purchases to those that we use as an ongoing reference; otherwise, we ask our town librarian to order books for us through the inter-library loan system.

Long ago, we stopped using paper tissues, napkins, and towels. I find it far more pleasant to pull a cloth handkerchief from my pocket—as my father and his father did—than a one-use paper tissue.

When Nancy and I hunger for carryout, we bring our own containers. Yes, it can be a bit awkward, just like when I tell the cashier at the hardware store that I don't need a bag, but I worry less and less about these uncomfortable moments. They pass quickly, while the trash we make can last for centuries. And I've found that when we take steps toward precycling, other people take note and do the same.

When I wanted to stop using a dishwasher, I got some flak. I was handed a "study" cut from a home and appliance magazine saying that dishwashers used less energy than washing by hand. This was clearly wrong, so I measured the amount of water and energy used in hand-washing and machine-washing dishes. No contest. Wash by hand. If you ever have a question like this, borrow a Watts-Up meter from your county extension office.

A similar false claim was made when I took our vacuum in to buy a replacement part. The salesman said the model we owned dated to 1961. Why didn't we buy a new one? It would be 200 percent more efficient, he said. The fact is that the motor on a new model draws over twice the amperage as the old model we inherited from Nancy's mom.

Knowing that all waste is eventually eaten or breathed, my family does not use plastic wrap or aluminum foil. This logic follows for so many products found around our home. For example, we use fewer than half a dozen cleaning products for clothes washing, dish washing, and housecleaning.

About five or six years ago, we stopped using a power mower to cut the lawn and switched to a push mower. Because our yard was too large to mow by hand, we let the backyard grow naturally, planted fruit trees, and put up a clothesline. One neighbor complained, but two others stopped mowing their backyards too.

When I read Butler's *Lives of Saints*, I marvel. Those heroes of God were stabbed, fried, mauled, impaled, dismembered, and burned as a witness to their love of Jesus. Their sacrifice did not drive others away from Christianity but toward it. Roman guards in charge of these martyrs were converted on the spot and gave up their own lives.

Hanging clothing on the line, giving up plastic wrap, and changing the lightbulbs are hardly equivalent to being burned alive as a human torch to light up one of Nero's parties. But even today, people, like the Roman guards, are drawn to anyone who believes in something enough to change their lifestyle.

Eventually my family moved to a smaller home; our old house was too big to be in line with our evolving values. Our new house is the height, width, and depth of our old garage. Our new house has no dishwasher, clothes dryer, garbage disposal, or garage, not to mention garage door opener. We mow no lawn. We grow fruit and maple trees, a vegetable garden, and wildflowers. Our new house is even more of a home base for our "world mission," and it is a place for ministry as well. It has become a place of sharing and prayer. We happily cram thirty people into our house for Wednesday-night faith group. Despite (and because of) our changed lifestyle, we look around and say, "We have too many things." The feeling is more urgent than when we lived in a big house. We still live better than nearly everyone else on the planet, and we are looking to downsize significantly again. A change has occurred. We used to leave two barrels of trash at the curb weekly. Yesterday, I took out a grocery-size paper bag that contained three weeks' worth of trash.

I do not think that anyone can say what the "right" size house is. Marta-Mary's crumbling shack was far more than many have, and by comparison, our current home is indefensibly large and luxurious. Each time we divest ourselves of possessions, we have fewer earthly things that bind us. My firsthand knowledge of the way Marta-Mary and one billion similar brothers and sisters live around this earth drives our family to do what we can to support them. I think about sleeping on cardboard and sticks when I am tempted by an ad for luxurious sheets and bedding. The changes we have made will not earn our way into heaven, but they do two important things for our souls: They connect us with the family of humanity around the globe, and, more important, they bring us closer to God. If he asks us to give up everything we have and follow him, I now know with certainty that each member of my family would gladly do so. This lack of attachment to things, rather than the size of our home, brings us priceless freedom and allows us to hear his call.

Chapter 12

It's a Wonderful Life

Paul, Lauren, Holly, Mike, and I sat around the main desk looking out over the vacant emergency room. It was late in the afternoon of Christmas Eve. We were throwing a pity party, imagining all the people we knew who were home with the snow gently falling, fireplaces crackling, and Bing Crosby singing in the background.

Workers from all over the hospital wandered by to join us. Occasionally, someone's spouse would remember us and call. Those of us who were on duty until the next morning looked with envy at those going home at eleven.

Ah, to be a tyke safely home in bed with visions of sugarplums dancing in our heads. Ah, to be a teacher and have two weeks off. Ah, to be anyone but us. We were stuck in a hospital, unable to leave.

At the height of our Christmas complaints, a man walked in accompanied by a girl in her early teens. "Is Dr. Sleeth here?" he asked. Holly pointed to me. "Hi, Dr. Sleeth," he said. "You don't know me. I'm Sam Marcus. This is my daughter, Katie. You took care of her in October." I didn't recognize the young teen all bundled up in an oversize parka; it's difficult to remember three thousand patients a year. So I nodded and smiled as Mr. Marcus offered me his hand.

"Katie is the one from the soccer game," he prompted. And then it came back to me. On a day that past fall, with the ER overflowing and unable to handle another case, a woman ran in and grabbed me by the arm. Every nurse was busy. I was talking on a wall phone with a hand over my free ear, trying to hear above the din of an intoxicated college student wrestling two nurses and a police officer.

Tugging at my sleeve was a frightened woman pleading for my attention. "There's a sick girl in my car. She won't wake up. Please help me," she begged.

I ran outside with her. A minivan was parked at an angle, blocking the ER entrance. Inside, a teenager slumped unconscious in the back.

"What happened?" I asked, unbuckling the girl.

"She was playing a great soccer game but then got sidelined."

"Did she get hurt?"

"No, she just said she didn't feel right."

I lifted the girl up and started carrying her into the ER. "Is she your daughter?"

"No, a neighbor's."

"Did she head a ball?" I asked.

"Yes, at the beginning of the game, when she kept the other side from scoring."

"Bingo," I said to myself.

Katie was completely obtunded (meaning that she was without any reflexes and unresponsive to any stimuli), and I fell into the "ABC" trauma approach: "Airway—intubate. Breathing—bag with 100 percent oxygen. Circulation—check the blood pressure, hang an IV. Disability—check for reflexes; none. Exposure—cut off an old sweatshirt and new soccer outfit, logroll her 360 degrees, and look for trauma."

A few moments in the CAT scanner confirmed a ruptured cerebral artery. I put in a call to the neurosurgeon. The radiologist and I watched as further images came up on the monitors. Beep. A tone came over a speakerphone, a call being relayed to the neurosurgeon's office. "This is the office of Bayview Neurological Associates."

"This is Dr. Sleeth in the ER. Who's on call?" I asked.

"Dr. Struck is on call today."

The radiologist sitting beside me made an exasperated face and shook his head.

"Who's in the office right now?" I queried.

"Dr. Diangio is. But he's not on call."

I picked up the hand unit of the phone to bypass the loudspeaker.

"Can I please speak to him anyway?" I persisted.

A few minutes later Diangio's calm voice came on. "What'cha got, Matthew?"

I explained about my thirteen-year-old patient.

"Am I on call?" he asked, knowing that he wasn't.

"No Bill, Dr. Struck is." I paused. "Bill, this girl's the same age as our kids. She's got an early bleed with no shift yet ..." He understood what I was saying. This wasn't the usual hopeless high-speed-head-versus-concrete case. This girl had a real chance, but she would lose it if left to his overcautious partner. Katie didn't need another CAT scan, an angiogram, and an MRI. She needed surgery. Now.

"You watch her for five minutes. I'll close the office and be right there," Diangio promised. He came and gave orders to prep for surgery. Later that night, Diangio stopped by the ER to say that the case had gone well. That was the last I'd heard of Katie until this Christmas Eve.

I finished shaking Mr. Marcus's hand and offered to shake Katie's. She stared at me shyly and took my hand.

"I'm sorry I didn't make it by earlier to thank you," Mr. Marcus apologized. "I've been so busy getting Katie back on her feet." He paused. "Eighteen months ago, my wife and oldest daughter were lost in a car crash. Katie is all I've got left," he said, and his voice began to falter. "Dr. Diangio told me what you did for Katie. I — I just want to thank you." He took in a great sob of a breath and gave up trying to control his voice or the tears that ran down his face. "You gave me the best Christmas present in the world. You gave me Katie." He opened his arms and hugged me. Then, overcome with emotion, he took Katie by the hand and left without another word.

The heavy door of the ER clanged shut. I looked around at the crew. Everyone was quiet, all complaints forgotten. Several wiped away tears. I pulled out my handkerchief and followed suit. Still it was quiet. Then Paul, a veteran nurse and father of two daughters, turned to me and quietly said, "It's a wonderful life."

It is a wonderful life, and perhaps no season holds more promise and joy than the Christmas season. It marks a moment in history that changed this wonderful world forever. This is the true significance of Christmas, when God became man, when the Word became flesh, when God gave his only begotten son — *this* changed everything.

Mr. Marcus put our self-absorption into perspective. He had lost two-thirds of his family, and we had been able to help save his Katie. It is perhaps one of the best Christmas presents I have ever been a part of. By coming in that Christmas Eve and sharing his tears and thanks, he gave to each of us in that room a Christmas present that we will always remember. Christmas is about giving. God gave his son to redeem humanity. Mary gave herself as a vessel for the Christ child, and the three wise men traveled from the East to give gifts to the Holy Family.

So it is not surprising that Christmas is synonymous with gift giving. It makes sense. It even makes sense that some of our gifts should cost money and be difficult to find or to deliver. Yet something has gone wrong with Christmas and gift giving.

The Christmas (or holiday) season has absorbed national and religious celebrations from Africa, the Far East, and now Islam. It has become a shopping black hole from which no event throughout November and December escapes. To further confuse the holiday, news reports are issued daily about the number of dollars spent between Black Friday (the Friday after Thanksgiving) and New Year's Day, and how this season's spending compares with last year's. We are left with a sense that it is our patriotic duty to worry about how the "nation's largest retailers" are faring. Christmas giving (spending) becomes another "economic indicator."

Christ was born in a barn. How did we go from a celebration of this humble birth to a season of frenzy, shopping, debt, depression, suicide, overeating, and blockbuster movie releases? Is it bad for us? Does it hurt the planet? Should we change?

These are difficult questions to answer. It seems that a complicated mixture of generosity, nostalgia, guilt, and perhaps unconscious confusion drives many people. Some of the confusion is between Santa Claus and Christ. It is a product of youthful memories, perceptions, and misconceptions. In our age of relativism, we have confused myth with religion. This blending of the two serves commercialism and shortchanges faith.

As adults, we sometimes take delight in our children's confusion and their misconceptions. When Clark and Emma were younger, their friends frequently ate lunch at our house. We never had any idea whether we would be serving two or six, which is why we often served spaghetti—it is an easy, expandable meal. Clark and his little friends would pronounce it "bisgetti." As they aged, their pronunciation naturally improved; however, one afternoon I realized that Clark, Emma, and their friends continued to ask for "Farmer John" cheese to sprinkle on the spaghetti. They were past the age when mispronunciation was an expected part of their speech. "What kind of cheese do you guys want?" I asked. "Farmer John," they answered. "Guys, it's called *Parmesan*." They disagreed with me. Two of them dashed to the refrigerator and returned.

"See," they said, "it's Farmer John." There on the round container was a farmer tilling a field on a tractor.

"Oh, I see how you got the idea," I said. Then I pointed to the label that said, "Naturally aged Parmesan cheese." They got it right away. (One wanted to know whether there was an unnatural aging process—but that's a different story.) Their misconception was easily righted. But what about the misconceptions children have that we don't know about or fail to correct?

Some uncorrected childhood misconceptions can be harmful, hurtful, and troublesome. Let me relate an example from my childhood.

As a first grader, I asked my mother one Saturday morning whether my father could stay home. This, I think you will agree, is not an uncommon request from a six-year-old.

"Why can't Dad stay home?" I wanted to know.

"I told you; he has to go to work," my mother replied.

"But why? Why can't he stay home?" I persisted.

"If your father doesn't go to work, he'll get fired," she said matter-of-factly. Then she turned away and resumed her task.

On one or two occasions, I had been with my mother when she had dropped my father off at his workplace, which was a military base. Uniformed soldiers in white helmets checked the identities of those entering the base. I had been fascinated that the guards wore real pistols. Now I knew why they were armed. If my father did not show up to work, one of those guards would drive to our house and "fire" him.

My six-year-old logic knew why my mother was annoyed at me for asking Dad to stay home. I had asked that he do something that would get him killed (fired). A wave of shame and fear overtook me. I went to my room and prayed that he would make it to work on time. For years afterward I felt relief when I heard him leave for work early in the morning.

Childhood misconceptions are ... well, childish. The one about Parmesan cheese became a joke with neighborhood children, and as teens they would ask Nancy or me to make spaghetti with "Farmer John cheese" on top. The misunderstanding about my father being "fired" for missing work was more serious. Eventually, one afternoon, as my father worked on a motor, I asked, "Do they still wear guns at the entrance of the base?" Because the moment was relaxed and my father was attentive, we quickly got to the bottom line: Being fired is not the same thing as being shot. Suppose when my father had realized my misunderstanding he hadn't straightened me out? Worse, what if he'd gone along with my flawed thinking? What if teachers, ministers, and media had failed to point me in the true direction?

Myth may or may not convey the truth. My children and I read C. S. Lewis's Narnia books aloud several times. They teach about good and evil, bravery and cowardliness. Our family adores the character of Reepicheep, but he and all the others in Narnia are a myth. If Clark or Emma ever asked, "Are they real?" we would say, "No, they're fictional characters the author made up to entertain and to teach." If any child asked a parent, teacher, or minister about the "realness" of the Narnia myth, he or she would be told what was real and what was not. No problem. Telling an eight-year-old that Reepicheep is a fictional character doesn't diminish the noble mouse's persona.

So what would you say if your eight-year-old asked, "Is Santa Claus real?" Would you hesitate to tell the truth? The rise in the prominence and "sacredness" of the Santa Claus myth directly coincides with the nation's emphasis on commercialism and its diminished belief in God. I do not know what is cause and what is effect, but I am concerned.

Consider the confusion that results in a young mind by the pairing of Santa and Jesus. Make a list and check it twice:

Do Santa and Jesus see you when you're sleeping? *Check.*

Both know if you've been bad or good? *Check.*

Both ask you to be good for goodness' sake? *Check.*

Both come to the forefront every December? *Check.*

Both symbolized by holly? *Check.*

Both able to fly? *Check.*

Both able to visit everyone in the world on a single night? *Check.*

Both ageless? *Check.*

Both pictured on Christmas cards exchanged by adults? *Check.*

Both soliciting donations for the poor? *Check.*

Both bringing gifts and holding children in special regard?
    Check.

Do parents, teachers, and ministers say both are real? *Check.*

Do children come to doubt their real existence? *Check.*

And this is the harm of the association. Because both are "sacred," a straightforward conversation about them is not allowed in public.

Santa Claus in his current form is quite new on the scene. He is the invention of a soft drink company that wanted to boost soda sales in the winters of the 1930s. Before that, he had a relatively small role. The real Saint Nicholas was a priest in ancient times who used his family money to rescue young women from prostitution and children from hunger.

Like so many parents, I lied to my children and told them Santa was real. I was told the same myth when I was a child. As adults we live with the memories of an idealized Christmas that amalgamated Santa and Jesus. Like many children, I came to doubt the existence of both. Why? How was I to discern when adults were lying and didn't mean it from when they meant something and were not lying? If lies are backed up with gifts and candy, and the truth with mere faith and promises, how does a six-year-old tell the difference? And why is Christ banished from the mall and not Santa?

Americans will spend about $750 per person this holiday shopping season. Think of what the impact would be if all this money was instead spent to do Christ's work. Since there are three hundred million of us in the country, we would have $225 billion to feed the poor, care for the sick, and clothe the naked. I can even see the rationale for going into debt to feed the hungry—but not to buy a separate set of Christmas dishes used once a year.

This is a dream we will probably never see. Yet the dream of a quiet, calm, spiritually renewing Christmas is within every believer's grasp. It can be a time of passing along the lesson of charity to our children.

Our family Christmas is relaxed. The children get a stocking and a book or small present. We make things for each other. All our decorations fit in a shoe-size box. We trim a houseplant —why cut down a tree, the symbol of Christ? Since they were little, Emma, Clark, and their friends have made popcorn chains to feed the deer and birds. We read Luke's Christmas story aloud, as well as a few other favorite children's books. It takes only a short while to pull apples, a few small presents, and chocolate out of their stockings, and yet I think my children enjoy Christmas more than most teenagers.

A group of Anabaptists dropped by our house last year in mid-December. One of the beautiful little girls looked up at me, her hair under a scarf, her cheeks flushed from being out in the snow. She was so excited she couldn't get her words out. Her mother put her arm around her daughter's shoulder and said, "She's nervous because of Christmas. We don't have lights or trees or go shopping —we love Jesus so much that we get excited about his birth." One of the teens spoke with great animation about how they would worship on Christmas Day. It is not that children like these are "good" because they don't expect dozens of presents. It's because they haven't grown up getting so many things that they're happier.

Every year, we give each other less and less, yet I look forward to Christmas more and more. I do not have to try to re-create a fantasy Christmas from my youth. Last year, shortly before Christmas, I looked at the sweater Nancy wears at home. It is one that her father handed down and that she "adopted" as a teenager. I call it her Saint Francis sweater. It has dozens of holes and spots where it's been mended. The Salvation Army would throw it in the trash.

I looked at Nancy and asked, "Do you want a new sweater for Christmas?"

"No," she said. "I have a few for work, and this one for home." She gave me a kiss. "All I want for Christmas is your love." It is wonderful to be married to a woman who says this and truly means it.

Do America's living rooms overflow with presents because we

really need them, or out of a need to impress, or from a sense of guilt and obligation? Would a calm, divinely centered, debt-free, peaceful Christmas do us more good than a buying spree on credit? Instead of exchanging gifts in the workplace, why not take up a collection to give farm animals to poor people, plant trees in devastated countries, or provide health care to orphans? The spirit of giving that comes through the example of Jesus is about meeting the spiritual and material needs of others. Do you or your spouse need another sweater, tie, or scarf more than a child in Bosnia or Iraq needs a pair of good-fitting shoes?

A wonderful life isn't about having more; it's about appreciating what we have and sharing our abundance. One gift that means a great deal and costs nothing is the gift of thanks. It is said that gratitude is not only the greatest virtue but the mother of all others. This Christmas, write a thank-you letter to your spouse, children, parents, minister, and teachers—and visit the hospital on Christmas Eve if the staff there has saved a family member's life.

Chapter 13

Power and Light

Paul LeFontane was working late in his woodshop. He had a contract to build kitchen cabinets, and they had to be delivered by the following week. Exhausted, Paul ripped a last board on his table saw, leaned under, and switched off the motor. He was finally through for the day. His production schedule was tight, but Paul was going to make the deadline. He glanced at the saw's rip fence and found a small chip, one-inch square, littering the area. Without thinking, he brushed it away with the back of his right hand, which came into contact with a twelve-inch carbide-tipped blade still spinning at a thousand rpm.

Paul swore at his absentmindedness, but as he later told me, he didn't break the third commandment. He looked at the back of his hand. It didn't seem so bad. The inch-long cut didn't look deep, and it wasn't bleeding much. He wrapped the blue bandana he kept in his overalls around it, switched off the shop lights, and walked across the yard to his home. It was only when Carol, his wife, went to bandage the cut that he realized something else was wrong: He couldn't raise his index finger. Carol said that they should go to the emergency room, but he hesitated. As a self-employed farmer and cabinetmaker, he lacked health insurance. He and Carol are the kind of people who pay their bills out of pocket, and they take their bills seriously.

I examined Paul's hand under the bright glare of a surgical light. Upon finding the severed end of the index finger's extensor tendon, I gently pulled. Out stretched his index finger, just like the one in Michelangelo's creation of Adam on the Sistine Chapel's ceiling.

"You'll need a few stitches in the tendon to bring it back together," I said. "We'll get the orthopedic or plastic surgeon on call to do it."

"How much will that cost?" they wanted to know.

"If the orthopod does it here in the ER, my guess is it will run about $1,500 to $2,000. If it's the plastic surgeon, he'll insist on doing everything in the OR. Then it will probably run you $5,000 to $8,000."

They sat in stunned silence. Then Carol asked, "Can you stitch it?" I cleared my throat and did the famous doctor stall: "Hmmm." I've never had a malpractice complaint. Part of the secret of never being sued is doing fewer procedures than you were trained to do. But part of being a worthwhile human being is doing more than you "feel" like doing.

"Sure, I can do it. We used to reattach extensor tendons in the ER, and the only reason we don't still is fear of malpractice."

"How much will you charge to do it?" asked ever-practical Carol.

"I'm a hospital employee, so I don't know the exact charges, but they're gonna bill you for seeing me anyway. Depending on how I dictate the case ... maybe $200 or $300." After I gave them the litany of what could go wrong and explained that Paul would be in a cast for six weeks, they still urged me to repair the tendon.

In five minutes, I had both severed ends of the tendon exposed and was starting to place the first stitch when everything went black as night.

"Power outage," I said in the dark. At that moment, the explosive recoil of the generator could be heard outside in the parking lot, and in another split second the lights came back on. I finished up.

We chatted some more, and they asked me where I lived. "What time do you get off work?" Carol asked.

"Not until eight tomorrow morning."

"Can you drop by our place? We're right on your way home. I can make you some breakfast," she offered. I was familiar with their farm, and we made a date.

The emergency power from the generator is not distributed equally throughout the hospital. The ICU, OR, and ER get all they want. The patients' rooms, cafeteria, and other areas get only enough to power emergency lights. The grid was down the remainder of the night, so the hospital ran off its generator. Every time someone came through the ER entrance, the noise of the generator rose, and in billowed the smell of its diesel fumes.

In the morning, I stopped by the LeFontane farm. After breakfast, they gave me a tour. They had built their house, two barns, chicken coop, and woodshop themselves. As we walked toward the shop, Paul introduced me to Pete and Repeat, the Percheron draft horses they used for farming. They were huge, beautiful creatures with a combined weight of three thousand pounds. "Yup," Paul said, "you're looking at two horsepower."

The LeFontanes use these horses to do all the plowing, cultivating, cutting, towing, and harvesting on their forty-acre farm. They use them to move snow in the wintertime. Pete and Repeat seem to enjoy hauling around a hay wagon and thirty to forty adults and children when the LeFontanes host their church's annual Fourth of July picnic.

To understand how much power we consume, it's useful to consider Pete and Repeat. Power used to come in units that made sense, and in terms a human could relate to. A one-horsepower motor is capable of the same amount of work as one draft horse. That's where the term *horsepower* comes from.

Power is something people love. We just don't seem to be able to get enough of it. My four-year-old Honda Insight is a gratuitous display of a power-hungry world. It has seventy horsepower. Seventy—the equivalent of seventy Pete and Repeat draft horses! It has the power to haul 1,400 church picnickers. It will go from zero to "speeding ticket" in ten seconds. It gets only about fifty-four miles to the gallon.

I recently saw a truck ad that appeals to the basest desires of humankind. It shows the grill of the vehicle covered in dead insects. The butterflies, grasshoppers, ladybugs, and fireflies "lose," proclaims the ad. You "win" by having the power to kill anything in your way. When a butterfly or bird ends up dead on your truck, it dies "a more noble death."

The average SUV has 210 horsepower. To get that in perspective, the largest yellow school buses have the same horsepower and carry ninety adults. If pulled by 210 real horses, wagons carrying over eight thousand people could be hauled with the same horsepower as an average SUV.

Imagine the mighty draft horses Pete and Repeat hitched to a grinding wheel, going round and round. But let's replace the grinding wheel with a modern electric generator. How much electrical energy could they produce? And what would it run? One horse can generate about 750 watts. Pete and Repeat yoked together could make 1,500 watts, or 1.5 kilowatts. (1,000 watts = 1 kilowatt; energy at the rate of one kilowatt for one hour = 1 kilowatt-hour; 1 horsepower = 746 watts.)

If a family had a generator wheel with two draft horses hitched up and walking in a circle, it could operate a 1,500-watt appliance

—a hair dryer, for instance. The family could not operate a clothes dryer, which requires 5,000 watts. It would take seven draft horses —or well over five tons of Percherons pulling in unison—to dry a load of laundry.

An appropriate symbol of a home that cares about God and his creation could be the clothesline, the simplest and perhaps oldest passive-solar device. Most of the ones around here are built like mine—two four-by-fours sunk in the ground with two two-by-sixes attached horizontally across the top of each. Each end of the clothesline looks like a cross. Two crosses with $3 worth of line strung between them make a solar-powered clothes dryer. Yesterday, in early November, I hung a load on the line around noon and brought it in before dinner, fresh and dry.

All across the country, people are getting worried about America's power supply. We've been reminded of our vulnerability because of planned brownouts and blackouts, unplanned power failures, and disruptions to the grid due to catastrophic weather. We've also learned that the supply of oil is not inexhaustible. No one is quite sure when it will run out, but no one is saying that it will last forever, either. And there are many indications that oil will be in short supply sooner rather than later. About 70 percent of our nation's electricity is generated by fossil fuels, 20 percent by nuclear power, and all but the remaining 1 percent from hydropower. America's alternative energy consists of solar, wind, geothermal, biomass, and methane. All of the alternative sources together account for only 1 percent of our electric power supply, and we have been developing these sources for three decades.

When America meets the challenge of power shortages in its near future, it will not do so through new space-age power sources, although they may help. It will do so through efficiency and conservation.

Fifteen years ago, we had 60-watt incandescent lightbulbs in our home. We replaced these with 11-watt compact fluorescent bulbs. Now we are beginning to change over to 1.5 watt LED bulbs. It is always cheaper, easier, and better for the planet to save energy than to try to make it. The average home uses over 1,000 kilowatt-hours of electricity a month. Our average is less than 150 kilowatts. I hope to get that down to about 100. Furthermore, we did not lower our electric bill by "robbing Peter to pay Paul," —we did not switch from an electric clothes dryer to a gas one or an electric refrigerator to a propane one and then think that we were "saving."

In the wintertime, we hang our clothing indoors along the south-facing windows. Hanging laundry in the dry winter air has the bonus of moisturizing the air in our house without plugging in a humidifier. The clothesline is on a retractable reel. When a neighbor stopped by the house the other day to deliver a church calendar, I had a momentary feeling of embarrassment about the clothes hanging on our indoor line. Why? Because we do not picture our nation's leaders, university presidents, and mega ministers hanging their family's undergarments up to dry. Why? Because it would make them look less powerful. Power is a symbol of wealth, and wealth is symbolized by power.

Every time my family used the electric clothes dryer, we put five pounds of greenhouse gases into the air. It is interesting that we didn't feel embarrassed about our pollution or expenditure of money and nonrenewable resources. Equipment that uses power projects the modern image of wealth, and vice versa. Perhaps this is why so many people ride to the mall in a three-thousand-pound vehicle using the equivalent of two hundred horses to pull it. We may not be in charge of the country, but we can drive a vehicle befitting a presidential motorcade.

I am certain that if Christ were alive today, he would hang his and the disciples' clothing on the line to dry. The resemblance of a clothesline to a cross would not embarrass him. Jesus was the kind of power source that could feed five thousand with just a few fish and a couple of loaves of bread. Power and wealth: What does Jesus have to say about them?

> Come to me, all you who are weary and burdened, and I will give you rest. Take my yoke upon you and learn from me, for I am gentle and humble in heart, and you will find rest for your souls. For my yoke is easy and my burden is light. (Matthew 11:28–30)

If we are tired, weary, distressed, hurt, sad, overworked, or underappreciated, we are to come to him. He will give us rest. Rest, peace that passes human understanding, calmness of spirit, stillness of heart—these are his offerings to us. But there is a condition: We are to take his yoke upon us, to take up his work, his Word as our word, his leadership as our leadership. What kind of Lord is he? He is gentle, humble, thoughtful, and kind.

The power of God is power in a new and sublime form. The world is fixated on other power: horsepower, megawatts, kilotons of TNT, and rads of nuclear energy; dollars, euros, yen, securities, and bonds. Christ walked everywhere he went. He befriended women, children, lepers, and prostitutes. With the power of God, everything gets reversed and turned upside down. A family that dedicates itself to a mission of saving energy and giving the money to charity can hardly claim trophies or reserved parking spaces at the club. They are opting for a different kind of power. When I bring a sandwich to work in a reusable container, am I concerned that it will make me look weak, or poor, or powerless? When I worry about what the world thinks, I disconnect from the power of heaven.

This afternoon, I walked into the woods to be alone with God. The trees, ferns, birds, and squirrels were already glorifying the Lord, so I kept quiet and joined them. I did not trouble him with my requests; he gets enough of them. I simply sat, and listened, and let my worldly thoughts stop raging. I heard the stream. Then I heard the highway, and immediately my thoughts raced to how I wished I were wealthy enough to live in the middle of a hundred-acre farm, far from the highway noise. But then I let go of that wish; after all, where I live is a million times closer to nature than most of the world's homes. Quiet. Peace. A yoke that fits. "I will give you rest" sounded as a few snowflakes fell in the weak afternoon sun of late autumn. "Learn of me; I will teach you to be humble and gentle," the small stream seemed to urge.

The Bible says that when we get to heaven there will be no sun, no candles, no lights. God himself will illuminate the vast eternity of heaven. Even here on earth, his source of power is available to us. It simply does not come in octane or kilowatt ratings. Because power and light are so central to both faith and environmentalism, in the back of this book (appendix B) I've included a nuts-and-bolts discussion of the question I'm most often asked: How did my family get our average monthly electrical bill down to $20?

The "things" that run on electricity are more numerous than the visible stars in the sky. All the generations of man prior to a century ago lived out their lives without these items. My grandmother advised: "Take care of the pennies and the dollars will look after themselves." It is much the same when it comes to electrical consumption. Once you care enough to unplug the clock in the spare bedroom, you probably won't run out and buy a two-hundred-gallon saltwater aquarium, a lava lamp, or anything else without asking, "Will this bring me closer to God?"

Chapter 14

First,
Do No Harm

I have some good news and some bad news. Enormous strides have
been made in the areas of public health, surgery, and medicine.
The blind are made to see. The deaf can hear through cochlear
implants. Smallpox has been wiped off the earth. Diphtheria, teta-
nus, pertussis, polio, and even chicken pox can be prevented with
immunizations. But one public health statistic remains stubbornly
unchanged. It hasn't budged since the time of Jesus. The death
rate remains at an amazing 100 percent. No matter how much
bran cereal you eat, how many miles you run, how high the good
cholesterol or how low the bad, you aren't getting out of this life
alive. And that's a fact.

Our culture seems to have difficulty accepting a death rate of
100 percent. This is nothing new. Jesus talked about man's fear of
death and his tendency to cling to life. Jesus teaches that through
him we can expect an abundant and full life. Yet oddly, he says that
to do this, we must stop clinging to life.

Followers of Christ should be concerned with easing, treating, and healing the pain and suffering of others. However, we
are bound by a covenant not of life in this world, but in looking
forward to life in the next. The day of one's death is better than
that of birth (Ecclesiastes 7:1). The closer I draw to the day of my
death, the more I long for it. I enjoy being alive as much as anyone,

FIRST, DO NO HARM

but I long to see my Lord, and just as Jesus promises, I find that life grows sweeter when I cling to it less.

Our national obsession with health is unhealthy. I have talked to many doctors who have encountered the following scenario in dealing with terminally ill patients. The physician presents option one: no heroic efforts, just pain management and comfort care. Then option two is presented: chemotherapy, medical therapy, surgery, radiation — the spare-no-expense-with-little-hope-of-a-cure approach. Often, patients or their families say, "I don't care what it costs; I want everything done." In a world of infinite resources, this would not matter; it would be simply a personal choice. But we live in a world of finite resources, and the resources available are unevenly distributed.

There's a pop song called "Blue Monday." It wails, "Oh how I hate blue Mondays." The health-care industry has claimed blue Mondays; Monday is 14 percent of a seven-day week, just as health care represents about 14 percent of our economy. Every Monday of every week of every month of every year of everyone's life equals the cost of medicine in the United States. Is that too much?

Anything that takes up the equivalent of one day a week deserves our careful and prayerful consideration in light of its overall material, spiritual, and eternal impact. When we face a dilemma, begin by asking, "Will it bring me closer to God?" Then we must ask, "Can I live in a culture that does not use God as a moral compass without being swayed or distracted?" These are critical questions that individuals and families, rather than governments and corporations, must ask about health-care issues.

Let's compare two real people based on the current worldview of health. Patient A and Patient B are both well-known authors who also dabble in painting. Patient A is a nonsmoker and a nondrinker. He maintains his ideal body weight. He sees his doctor for regular checkups and follows the advice he is given. On his doctor's recommendation, he exercises daily and gives up high-cholesterol foods entirely. Also on his physician's recommendation, he eats, vacations, and sleeps according to a regular routine.

Patient B is four inches shorter than Patient A and weighs one hundred pounds more. He is a lifelong smoker and drinker and adores high-cholesterol foods. He exercises sporadically, but only when he feels like it. He often stays up until three in the morning; sometimes he sleeps until noon. He doesn't trust doctors and rarely takes their advice. Even after a major heart attack, he refuses to quit smoking, drinking, or eating eggs for breakfast. He doesn't take medications prescribed for high blood pressure, and he returns to work forty-eight hours after his heart attack.

Think for a moment about Patient A and Patient B. Which would you want as a neighbor, son-in-law, or president? Only in a culture blinded by superficial physical fitness could we believe that we know about either patient's character or morality.

Most people are surprised to learn that "good" Patient A is Adolph Hitler and "bad" Patient B is Winston Churchill. It is Churchill, and not Hitler, who believed in God. Churchill's faith, courage, and moral compass were unwavering. In one of his books, Churchill describes what light and color will be like in heaven; heaven is the place Churchill set his eyes on. And only heaven knows where democracy and the world would be today if Churchill had been the sort of man who worried about his waistline or heeded his doctor's advice.

What do Americans get for their health-care dollars? Rounded to the nearest hundred dollar, every man, woman, and child spends $5,000 on health care annually. A woman's life expectancy in the United States today is seventy-nine years. In comparison, Mexico spends about $500 a person on health care, and a woman's life expectancy there is seventy-six years. That's $400,000 in total life-time expenditures for the American versus $38,000 for the average Mexican woman—a bundle of money for only three more years of life. Compared to a vast portion of the world's people, Mexico has a posh health-care budget. Virtually no country in all of Africa has a budget of $100 per capita for annual health care. Americans spend more on dog and cat health care than Africans spend on human health care.

Let's return to the mountains of Central America. On this particular day, four doctors have gathered in a two-room school to hold a clinic. Dr. Andrews, an oral surgeon, has set up a portable dental chair and bottles of bleach to sterilize tools. He has a battery-powered headlight on. His teenage sons are assisting him, and he will do dental extractions the entire day. He will go and go until he says he can do no more, and then the line of people waiting to see him will have to go without, or hope that he will take just a few more of the worst cases. On this day, he will pull 104 teeth. Running out of novocaine will not stop him—or the crowd. They will insist he pull their painfully decaying teeth anyway.

We see patients for three hours and then Katie, an interpreter on our team, suddenly is overcome with fever, chills, and vomiting. She insists we keep working and rests under a shade tree for the remainder of the day. We check on her often. The moment one of us decides she is seriously ill we can put an evacuation into motion. Our insurance policy will pay to get us on a jet and back to a hospital in Miami should the need arise. No expense will be spared to help a member of our American medical team.

And then I meet the Yarmatiez family, or at least most of them. The eldest child is at home with his father. The next three siblings have respiratory infections with fevers and wheezing. Mother says

SERVING GOD, SAVING THE PLANET

they have been this way for two weeks. They are losing weight. I give them all antibiotics. What they need is a chimney to carry the smoke from the stove above their roof. Without a chimney, these children "smoke" the equivalent of three packs of cigarettes a day.

The fifth Yarmatiez child is a boy. He is sick with the same respiratory infection, but he has had it longer, is losing more weight, and is working hard just to breathe. Mrs. Yarmatiez also inquires about whether anything can be done to fix his right eye.

"How old are you?" I ask him.

"Cinco," he manages to whisper.

A thick, opaque white membrane covers his right eye. It has been this way for a year and a half. A ball scratched his cornea, and lacking five minutes of initial treatment, he is permanently blind in the eye.

I place my left hand across his thin, huffing chest to steady him while I press my stethoscope to his back. The little muscles between his ribs retract each time he takes a breath, and I hear a loud mechanical wheezing followed by a high-pitched squeaking on the next cycle. His tiny chest feels hot. His temperature is 103. He needs antibiotics, but he also needs an inhaler to treat his asthma. I hesitate. We did a count this morning, and we have only two inhalers left. And we will be seeing patients here for at least three more days.

Think about spending the next week breathing through a straw —not the big kind that McDonald's hands out by the billions, but the small kind that is used to stir coffee and then thrown away. That is what it is like to have untreated asthma. Now add pneumonia, a fever, blindness in one eye, and hunger to the symptoms. I gave the five-year-old Yarmatiez boy one of our inhalers.

Next came his four-year-old and eighteen-month-old sisters. "Do they have fevers and coughs as well?" I ask. No, thankfully they do not. Then Mother describes the four-year-old's symptoms. Every day she has a seizure. On some days, she has two or three. These convulsions started when she was a year and a half. She is not developing normally. She doesn't talk or seem to hear what her mother says. "Was she normal until the seizures began?" I ask.

"Yes."

We have no seizure medicines to offer her. I apologize, "There is nothing I can do to help her."

"And how about the little one?" The little girl looks coyly at me, leaning against her mother. Her eyes are brighter and more curious than her big sister's. But in the past month, she too has begun having seizures. I feel helpless.

Mrs. Yarmatiez is also concerned about her husband, who was unable to walk the half hour here with the rest of his family. He has had pain for three days. It hurts in his flank. He cannot find a comfortable position. He is urinating blood. "A kidney stone" is my long-distance diagnosis, and I send a donated half-full bottle of pain medicine home with her.

She has one last question. Do I have any birth control? We do not. I cannot help her. She nods her head in acceptance. What else can she do? She must accept a husband in pain, a daughter whose brain is being slowly eroded by uncontrolled seizures, the prospect of another child who will follow the same course, a son who is blind in one eye and slowly dying of asthma, and the inevitability of another mouth to feed in the coming year.

Whenever a doctor writes about patients, he must change the sex, age, location, or disease to protect confidentiality. I have done this throughout this book, but with this family I have changed only the name; every other detail about the pain and suffering of this family of nine is all too real. Yet they remain anonymous because there are more than a billion like them in the world. Their situation reminds me of the parable of the rich man and Lazarus:

> Jesus said, "There was a certain rich man who was splendidly clothed and who lived each day in luxury. At his door lay a diseased beggar named Lazarus. As Lazarus lay there longing for scraps from the rich man's table, the dogs would come and lick his open sores. Finally, the beggar died and was carried by the angels to be with Abraham. The rich man also died and was buried, and his soul went to the place of the dead. There, in torment, he saw Lazarus in the far distance with Abraham.
>
> "The rich man shouted, 'Father Abraham, have some pity! Send Lazarus over here to dip the tip of his finger in water and cool my tongue, because I am in anguish in these flames.'
>
> "But Abraham said to him, 'Son, remember that during your lifetime you had everything you wanted, and Lazarus had nothing. So now he is being comforted, and you are in anguish. And besides, there is a great chasm separating us. Anyone who wanted to cross over to you from here is stopped at its edge, and no one there can cross over to us.'" (Luke 16:19–26 NLT)

I think of this parable when I contrast medicine in the United States with that of the third world. Our unused and outdated medicines are the difference between life and death for them. Our out-of-style glasses are the difference between them seeing clearly or experiencing life as a blur. We inject minute amounts of botulism toxins to treat age lines, while they die young from not being able to stop botulism. America is constantly tearing down and rebuilding perfectly usable hospitals, while they have none.

As individuals, what can we do to help? First, seek the kingdom of heaven. If you are scared to death of dying, you are not right with God. Billy Graham said publicly that he is tired. He doesn't want any dazzling medical care. He wants to be able to go home and see his Lord. Reverend Graham is right with God, the definition of a life well lived.

Everyone should have a firm grip on the reality of his own end time. It amazes me how many families have never discussed the outcome of all life: death. My family doesn't sit around the dinner table planning our funerals, but when a guest brings up the subject of end-of-life care, we do have a family gag about rehearsing the "eye signals."

I start by quizzing Clark and Emma. "What do you do if I'm paralyzed and can't talk, and I signal you like this?" I blink one eye rapidly.

"Pull the plug," says Emma.

"Right! Now how about if I give this signal?" I close my eyes and keep still. Clark and Emma go into a whispered huddle as the guests await the answer.

"Pull the plug, right?" Clark half says, half asks. Then Emma agrees, "Yes, I think that eye signal means pull the plug."

"Super! And this one?" I ask, keeping both eyes wide open.

"That's a definite pull the plug," they chime in unison.

You get the point. And so do my children. They know that I am not afraid to go to my Maker when the time comes for him to call me home.

I have found, without exception, that the closer a family is, the more comfortable they are letting go of terminally ill members. It is estimated that 30 percent of all the health-care dollars spent in the United States are spent during a person's last twelve months of life. The real waste is not the money spent on futile efforts but the medical distractions that keep families from saying "I love you" or

"Thank you, Mom" or "Will you forgive me, Dad?" The family becomes trapped in the medical system, and taking its cues from that system, family members often fail to admit reality. They end up missing opportunities to share love and gratitude and forgiveness during their few remaining moments on earth.

The last days of life can be a time of forgiving and of laying aside perceived and actual wrongs. It is the last chance to get the meaning of "love one another" right. Parents and spouses who are informed of your wish to go without any extraordinary measures are much more at peace supporting that decision if it is discussed in person, and well in advance. The end of one's life should reflect the same values of charity, thoughtfulness, and universal brotherhood as any other phase of life. If left to "the system," that system will look to its own interests.

If at all possible, make sure you have a doctor who realizes that pain and suffering are the enemy, and that death is not. Death is not your failure, or the doctor's, but the first chapter of eternity. I have attended many deaths, and I have witnessed that true believers are the people who live right up until the moment their soul leaves their bodies. They impart a sense of peace, purpose, and continuity to a world desperate for meaning. The same is true for how they handle disease and illness at all stages in their life. They do not harass their doctors for a CAT scan or an MRI just because their back has been hurting for three days. They have confidence in others because they have confidence in the future. This confidence grows from knowledge of God and a peace with things beyond their control. People who are comfortable with their mortality understand that it is God who calls the shots.

One factor that contributes to the ill health of much of the third world is wealthy-consumer demands for the factory-like exploitation of natural resources. Educating ourselves about products that are hurting or helping our third-world neighbors is a step toward our "home mission." With every place on the planet a few hours' flight away, Lazarus sits at all of our doorsteps. Changing our lightbulbs and driving less sends him clean air. Buying organically grown coffee, tea, and bananas gives him clean water. We must heed Jesus's commandment to love one another—to care for the billions of Lazaruses across the globe—before our time on earth runs out.

Chapter 15

Population Fallout

I keep in my desk two letters that I received within a week of each other. A minister wrote the first letter I received. I'd seen his daughter late one night for serious complications of diabetes. His child progressed rapidly into a condition called diabetic ketoacidosis. Such episodes carry a significant mortality risk. The minister's letter went something like this:

> *Dear Doctor Sleeth,*
>
> *You're the greatest. We've seen hundreds of doctors, but you were kinder, more knowledgeable, and better at explaining what you were doing than anyone we've ever seen. . . .*

It was a nice letter, the kind that makes me feel all warm and fuzzy, so I kept it. The other letter was from a newspaper journalist who had been in an auto accident years before. The accident had left her with multiple chronic and painful problems. I saw her for one of these recurring problems. Her letter went something like this:

> *Dear Doctor Sleeth,*
>
> *I have seen hundreds of doctors, and you are the worst ever. If I had anything to do with it, you would not be allowed to trim the toenails of a rabbit. You are the most insensitive, poorly trained, and*

*arrogant person it has been my misfortune to meet. You are a shame
to your profession. How a medical school could graduate you . . .*

When I read this letter, I felt like someone had thrown a spear
through my heart. So I kept it.

The first letter was easier for me to read, but it was harder to
learn anything from it. The second letter, however painful, forced
me to self-reflect. I reviewed the journalist's relevant medical
records in order to understand as fully as possible what I could
have done differently and why I had failed to meet her expecta-
tions. Even if my medical care had been flawless, I needed to face
the fact that I had failed to connect with the patient in this case.
Facing stern and unpleasant facts is a "biblical lesson" that we must
all learn.

It is often said that the Bible shows history "warts and all."
Its method of recording history and giving instruction is unusual
when compared to that of other ancient cultures. For example,
the Egyptians wrote detailed histories on their monuments and
temples. We can still read of their clashes with the Nubians, Phoenicians, and others. But never do they record themselves losing
a battle; the historians simply report that they won battles closer
and closer to home. The history of the Assyrians, Babylonians,
and Phoenicians follow suit. They sound like modern-day boxers:
"We're the greatest. No one beats us. All enemies fall before us."
This is the "truth" of other cultures, a "that's-my-story-and-I'm-
sticking-to-it" type of reality.

The Bible is different. From the Old Testament to the Gospels,
through the book of Acts and into the Epistles, the Bible reveals
prophets and church leaders blundering while searching for the
truth. Its authors record mistakes of friend and foe alike. In the
book of Exodus, Moses doesn't edit his ready-fire-aim method of

dealing with situations; he exposes his mistakes so that others can learn from them.

One argument for the truth of the Bible is its unique tradition of, well, telling the truth. Who would make up a patriarch who lies about his wife being his sister, a prophet who preaches stark naked, and an apostle who talks until a listener falls out of the window?

The Bible tells us to examine life and deal with the truth. We are not to turn our heads or try to "edit" the facts. Jesus says, "Be ye therefore wise as serpents, and harmless as doves" (Matthew 10:16 KJV). This millennia-old tradition of discussing and disclosing all the facts is a powerful tool that results in survival. The Assyrians, Nubians, and Babylonians are long gone, yet the Hebrews and Christians remain alive and well.

With this biblical search for the truth in mind, I have given a lot of thought to the topic of population, a subject many would prefer to ignore, deny, or sweep under the rug. Yet it is a subject that must be discussed in both an environmental and a biblical context. Following are some of the most common misconceptions I frequently hear.

America doesn't have a large population.

False. America is the third most populous country on the planet. Only China and India have more people.

America's population has stabilized.

False. When I was growing up, we had about two hundred million citizens. Now we have three hundred million. At our current rate of growth, in seventy years we will reach six hundred million. America has the highest population growth rate of any industrialized country.

*Most of America's increase in population is a result
of immigration.*

False. We have high immigration rates, but the majority of our growth still comes from domestic births.

Some countries are running out of people.

False. There are no countries running out of people. The media has reported that a few countries in what used to be the communist USSR have experienced population decreases as people are free for the first time to leave. But this handful of countries could easily increase their population by welcoming third-world immigration. Dig into these news stories and you will find issues of racial discrimination and attempts, by ruling ethnic and religious groups, to maintain control. You will also find the irresponsible handoff of intergenerational debt through underfunded retirement programs that rely on an ever-expanding population of workers.

Overpopulation is a global problem. If the children born between 2000 and 2005 were gathered on one island, that island would immediately be named the third most populous country in the world. On the flip side, not one island or acre of land has or can be added to this earth. As I travel around the country, I can see for myself the effects of population growth. The fields behind my boyhood home have sprouted "Woodfield Estates." Two-lane country roads are now six-lane highways. The streets of every major suburb are lined with cloned mega-box stores and chain-linked restaurants. Cities everywhere are becoming progressively more congested. This holds true around the globe. Countries that once depended on immigration for economic growth have slammed shut their doors.

I may not like statistics, but the Bible tells me to deal with them. Ours is the only sacred text that has an entire book devoted to facts and figures. In the book of Numbers Moses records a census of the Hebrew population.

Two thousand years elapsed between the time of Abraham and Jesus. During that time, the population grew steadily. Rome built paved roads from Ireland to Egypt. If the human population continued to increase at the rate it did then, our current global census would be one billion. Instead, we have 6.5 billion. What happened? The rate of population growth has changed. Picture this in terms of investing your retirement money at a rate of 1 percent versus 50 percent. You wouldn't need a calculator to compute which interest rate allows for an earlier retirement.

Another way of visualizing the rate of population growth is to take all of human history and place it on a twelve-month "Big Calendar of History." January 1st stands for the year 8000 BC. Each "day" represents twenty-seven years. December 31st on the Big Calendar of History represents the year AD 2000. Some important "days" are circled. In July, people start writing, building libraries, and using iron tools. In September, Christ lives, dies, and is resurrected.

December 24th is a big day. By now 98 percent of all human history has passed. On this day, the Census Bureau throws a party. Humanity has reached the one billion mark. On the 29th of December, we reach two billion. We add another billion on the 30th, and during the 31st we add a billion in the morning, another billion in the afternoon, and another billion before midnight.

If we continue at our current growth rate, placing a check on the calendar each time we add a billion more to the census, January of the next "Big Calendar Year" will have sixty million check marks. This means that there will be sixty million billion people on the earth by the month's end, or ten people for every square foot of earth.

Why the reluctance on the part of some people to face the fact that our current rate of growth is unsustainable? We should look at the possible reasons. Some might disagree with the facts themselves. I once heard a church representative claim that population problems are entirely made up. She offered the book *The Population Bomb*, written in 1968, as a prime example of mistaken data. In fact, however, *The Population Bomb* accurately predicted the world's census for the year 2000 to within an amazing 1 percent.

I find it difficult to argue with people who deny reality even when the facts are readily available. You can find census reports for the past century in libraries and online, and the government maintains at least two websites devoted to population statistics. Or you can check out the real-time population clock online, and then go back ten days later. Over 2,500,000 more people will have been added. Every two days, the earth adds half a million people. Every two days.

Some people discount population concerns because they advocate reproduction to advance their faith. Yet in his Great Commissioning, Jesus instructs the faithful to "go ye therefore, and teach all nations" (Matthews 28:19 KJV). We are to "teach," not out-procreate, all nations.

Humans were commanded by God to be fruitful and multiply. He bid the plants and the animals to do likewise. Yet, at some point any blessing can be overdone. God wants everyone to have enough to eat, but this does not mean he wants us all to be obese. Part of God's design for nature and humanity is to find a balance point of reason.

Some argue that population is a governmental issue and not appropriate for theological consideration. This is contrary to all of the Bible's teachings. Reproduction is a life issue and thus absolutely falls under the auspices of God. From the creation of Adam to the conception of Jesus, God has been involved in population issues.

Some people fear that population control will become linked to acts such as abortion. This is an argument that bears hearing and heeding. I do not believe that abortion has any place in birth control. My belief in the sanctity of life is the foundation for this book. If I did not hold unborn life as sacred, why would I work to improve living conditions for future generations? Preventing pregnancy, however, is not the same as aborting pregnancy. The two issues should be separate. One supports the dignity and welfare of the future; the other does not. If I don't work for a better tomorrow, I don't really believe in the sanctity of life.

Another argument is that the world has enough resources to feed and clothe everyone; the resources simply need to be distributed better. Resources can and should be better distributed; churches, governments, and businesses are working to do just that. But many countries double their populations in only thirty years. Even if the resources became available to end hunger today, poverty will reappear unless the number of mouths to be fed is stabilized.

The largest branch of Christianity believes that medical birth control is against "natural law." In the 1968 Papal Encyclical, the pope stated: "The Church calling them back to the observance of the norms of natural law, as interpreted by her constant doctrine, teaches that each and every marriage act must remain open to the transmission of life."

I do not believe that the Bible forbids us from using birth control. However, even if I did, the church's stand would be biblically sound *only* if it was based on a complete adherence to "natural law." To practice "natural law" a church or a family would have to accept both the natural birth rate *and* the natural death rate. The rate of population growth would have proceeded without problems if society had not introduced powerful, life-prolonging medicine. Modern medicine cannot be classified as "natural." Antibiotics, immunizations, Rh immune globulin, antimalarial medicines, and other drugs are made by humans. Medical interventions tamper with the "natural" death rate.

There are two biological and biblical oddities concerning human reproduction. First, the human female is the only mammal that is unaware of its day-to-day ability to conceive. Human females are unique in the animal kingdom because they regularly have sex when conception is impossible. Even "natural" family-planning techniques are built upon the unnatural availability of highly precise man-made thermometers and calendars. The second oddity is that humans have a higher "natural" death rate than any other mammal during childbirth.

I learned these biological facts before I knew the Bible well. In many ways, they make no sense—that is, until I examined the book of Genesis. There in chapter 3 is a passage so odd that many would dismiss it as a fable if it didn't happen to be true: "Unto the woman he [God] said, I will greatly multiply thy sorrow and thy conception" (Genesis 3:16 KJV).

Before the introduction of antibiotics, blood transfusions, surgical deliveries, anesthesia, antiseptic techniques, prenatal screenings, control of eclampsia, and use of forceps, one in five women died from a complication of childbirth. Go for a walk in a cemetery and examine the older gravestones. Why did all those women die in their twenties, thirties, and forties? Childbirth. Why, if they made it beyond menopause, did they often live until seventy or eighty? No childbirth.

The same statistics hold for children. Prior to 1900, it was commonplace for a family to lose half a dozen children. All the little monuments in my local cemetery are for infants who died of fatal ailments that my own children got "baby shots" to prevent. The little marble lambs on gravestones don't tell the whole story of past suffering, for these are only the graves of wealthy infants. Most babies were buried in anonymity with wooden crosses that have since decayed.

If the pope was indeed calling the faithful "back to the observance of the norms of natural law," that is a biblical mandate worthy of consideration. Natural birth and childhood, with their very high mortality, would quickly restore the natural balance of life and death. There would be no need for any birth control; indeed, controlling the birth rate would be counterproductive.

Returning to "natural law" means returning to families like that of John Wesley, the founder of the Methodist Church. His mother, Susanna, was one of twenty-five children. She and her husband, Reverend Samuel Wesley, had nineteen children. Ten died in childhood. Susanna considered herself blessed because nearly half her children survived until adulthood.

Christendom has chosen to ignore natural law in its most fundamental aspect: We forestall death. In so doing, we must take responsibility for our numbers. People say that "anything can be proven with the Bible." I don't think this is true, but taking one verse out of context, or magnifying one truth, is possible. That is why discussing earth stewardship cannot be reduced to an isolated issue.

If the earth's population were the same as it was just seven days ago on the "Big Calendar," we would have no global warming, cities with over a million people, or energy worries. There would still be elms on Elm Street and caribou in Caribou, Maine. We would marvel at the immense flocks of birds passing through blue skies. We would not require permits to hunt, fish, or cut trees.

As the population bomb explodes, the "fallout" is more state regulation to control fewer resources. Overpopulation inevitably leads to less freedom and access to enjoy God's created world. Our generation has the opportunity to peacefully disarm the population bomb. Ethically designed and distributed birth control is an essential remedy if humanity is to survive its own success.

Chapter 16

God Is Love

Doctors in training spend much of their time in a perpetual sleep-deprived state. Certain periods of my residency are one big blur. But I do remember a lesson I learned from a patient who had been sent to my floor by an attending physician. A brief note from the doctor asked me to "rule out dementia."

I shook hands with Bob Cicionni, a sixty-seven-year-old retired butcher. Bob was affable, and he asked me something patients rarely do. He wanted to know how I was doing.

"I'm fine," I said.

"That's funny," he answered. "You look a little tired and hungry."

I made a flippant remark — "I'll catch up on sleep in the next century" — and then refocused on him. "I have to ask you some questions. They might seem silly or insulting, too hard, or too simple, but if you indulge me, I can get an idea of how your memory is working."

"Okay, Doc, fire away," he said.

"First, I'm going to give you four words. You memorize them, and I'll ask you to repeat them in a few moments. Is that all right with you, Mr. Cicionni?"

"Sure, Doc."

I gave him the words. "In a few minutes I'll ask you for them," I reminded.

We got derailed when I found out he was an amateur local historian. He told me how he had picked up his love of history from his father, who had run a small newspaper. Eventually, an aide brought Mr. Cicionni his breakfast. "I can come back later and finish," I said.

"Fine, drop in anytime," he said. "Hey Doc, wasn't there something you wanted to ask me?"

"I don't think so," I replied.

"Sure, Doc, there was something."

"Oh, yeah," I remembered. "The four words. Can you recall them?"

"Ball," he said, and then hesitated.

"That's right; that's one of them."

"Ball ... and wagon."

"That's right; that's two of them."

"Wagon. Uhmmm ... did I say ball?" he questioned.

"Yes," I prompted. "You said ball and wagon."

"Hmm," he thought. "I give up, Doc. Can you tell me what the others were?"

"Okay, you said ball, right?" I asked.

"Yes," he encouraged. "I said ball and wagon."

I couldn't remember what came next. I'd been using the same four words for five years, and I couldn't bring them to mind.

"Don't worry, Doc. It'll come back to you." He smiled.

I stood there trying as hard as I could. When had I last used them? It was just two nights before, on call.

"Hey Doc," Bob interrupted my rumination. "They gave me two bowls of cornflakes. You want one? Go on, you look hungry, and I'm not going to eat both."

"Okay," I answered, still trying to remember.

"Sit down, Doc. Take a load off your feet," he graciously

offered. We sat there alone in the room with the sun pouring through the window. The room was strangely quiet. When Bob spoke, I realized I'd stopped chewing my cornflakes.

"You know, Doc, if something's important to you, you ought to write it down," he nodded at me. "You know why, Doc?"

"No, why?" I asked softly.

He smiled again, a patient teacher, unwilling to give up on me. "That way you won't forget it."

The most important truth in this world is sometimes the one thing that slips your mind. "Love one another" is Christ's new commandment. It supersedes all others, except to love God.

For me to love God, I must love all people. This book has been about the works we can do to save the next generation. Some may say that I've shortchanged faith. The argument about good works and their relative merit to faith is as old as the book of Acts. The Bible settles this issue: There is no faith without works, and no works without faith. It is like arguing the merit of my left hand versus my right as I flatten a piece of clay between them.

Christianity has an even odder concept than works versus faith. The Bible tells us that we must accept the lordship of Jesus in our hearts. This is not allegorical. We must allow God to set up shop in our heart, mind, and spirit. He wants us to move aside so that he can grow and grow until our hands become his hands and our words become his words. The farther one goes up this pathway, the more evident it becomes that God is the agent of all that is just and charitable in this world.

I am frequently asked about the nuts and bolts of living a less consumptive lifestyle: "How *exactly* did your family make a change?" I have tried to relate some of the steps we took, but the most important change is not the automobile you drive or the house you live in. What we need most is a change of heart.

Let's say that because of reading this book, you decide to change the lightbulbs in your home to compact fluorescents. The primary motivation may be your growing concern about the fumes from the power plant, or your desire to help a third-world asthmatic, or your hope to decrease a neighbor's chance of getting cancer. Or you may want to have a bit of extra cash to put in the collection plate. But what is really happening is a change of heart. You move over and make more room for God.

We are under strict instruction not to judge the motivation behind another's charity, for God is the source of all charity, and judging him is foolish. Christians believe that accepting Christ helps us learn to love. Once our act of rebirth occurs, we can get down to the business of doing what God has in store for us, and that by necessity involves "good works."

This is why Christ says, "Wherefore by their fruits ye shall know them. Not every one that saith unto me, Lord, Lord shall enter into the kingdom of heaven; but he that doeth the will of my Father which is in heaven" (Matthew 7:20–21 KJV).

We need to look at the significance of the wording "Lord, Lord" in this passage. Only a dozen times in its thousands of pages does the Bible repeat someone's name. God calls from a burning bush, "Moses, Moses here am I." Jesus stops the apostle Paul with "Saul, Saul why do you persecute me?" And Jesus corrects Mary's sister, "Martha, Martha," when she is harried with housework. Be assured: If God calls your name twice, you should stop what you are doing and pay attention. Saying a name twice is the Bible's way of showing profound intimacy. When Jesus says "Lord, Lord" in scripture, he is telling us that some people who know all about him will be barred from heaven. They may have said the sinner's prayer or have participated in all manner of Bible study and church worship, yet without the fruits of works, they cannot claim to have done the will of the Father. God may be on their lips, but they haven't made room for him in their hearts.

The "Lord, Lord" passage convicts me to search constantly for the will of God. Let me give an example. I have recently started wanting a dog. The thought of a golden retriever curled up by my desk as I write appeals to me. I grew up with dogs. I marvel at their simple joy in a walk. I began the subtle campaign for one. "Gee, Nancy, wouldn't it be nice to have a dog around the house?" But the real question is "Does God want me to do this?" There are many environmental reasons not to own a dog. But maybe they could be overlooked. Then two things happened. First, Nancy and I went for a walk. A neighbor's elkhound joined us on our stroll. On our return trip, he stopped, crouched, jumped three feet in the air, and came down muzzle first in a clump of grass. Up he sprang with a small rabbit in his teeth. I ran after him, but it was too late.

The next was a conversation Nancy had with some high-school students. What was the thing that most surprised newcomers to America? Her student from Italy said it was the size of our grocery stores. "You have aisles twenty meters long filled with animal foods!"

Two students from the Middle East were equally amazed at America's pet treatment. "You have animal hospitals—with emergency rooms!"

Should I get a golden retriever? I was being given my answer. Maybe I will be called to go somewhere next year but will hesitate because I own a dog. I don't know. The Bible doesn't say God has anything for or against the keeping of pets. But if I don't ask him, how will I know his will?

"Will this bring me closer to God?" It is a crucial question.

GOD IS LOVE

Even more important is "What does being closer to God mean?" It means that we love God and we love our neighbor as ourselves.

I have listened to many sermons in which the word love is never said. A booklet from the last church I visited has dozens of pages on the church's beliefs, bylaws, and constitution. It talks about creation, original sin, and redemption through Christ. These are all sound principles, but the booklet omits one crucial word: *love*.

Indeed, *love* has become a four-letter word. Love is not part of the rhetoric of global leaders, power brokers, or conglomerates. It does not make the evening news. It does not appear in medical journals. Popular books about love published over the past several decades reduce it to a biological act, a parody of positive and negative reinforcements, or a type of disease that one contracts but fades away like old blue jeans. Viewed this way, we must "fall in love" and hope that love's waters are deep enough to sustain us during the inevitable droughts.

Every quality except love has limitations. The apostle Paul in his famous love chapter (1 Corinthians 13) says that faith in God can move a mountain, but it won't get you into heaven. Giving everything to the poor won't get you in either. Love is the single most abiding force in the universe. The next best thing is charity, which also can be translated as "love."

Sarah Gower is a missionary in the mountains of Central America. When I grow up, I want to be like her. One morning, she asked if I would take a look at a neighbor. Sarah is not the kind of person that I can refuse. So off we went, walking down the road. We passed through multiple gates while chickens, goats, and little children raced about.

After climbing a narrow, steep walkway, we came to a typical mud and stick house. She introduced me to Michael and his family.

I had been warned that Michael was bitten on the leg by a

spider as an eighteen-year-old. Over the past twenty-five years the wound had not healed. Several missionary doctors had attempted treatments. I looked at his right leg. The closest analogy I can use is that of a tree after a beaver has gnawed on it. Above his mid-calf, his leg appeared normal. Below, an area of raw meat narrowed down toward the bone, as if it had been chewed away.

Michael's last visiting doctor had told him to soak the extremity in a five-gallon bucket with water and bleach. These daily treatments had helped a little, but the decades-old festering wound still had not healed.

Getting leg wounds to heal has been a minor hobby of mine. Using Sarah as an interpreter, I explained, "Arm wounds always heal. Why don't leg wounds? The way to make a leg wound heal is to turn it into an arm." I held one hand high above my head and let the other hang low for thirty seconds. Then I displayed both arms to the patient so he could see the difference in blood flow and drainage.

Michael got it. His wife got it, as did Sarah. For twenty-five years, he had been doing the wrong thing to heal the leg; he needed to keep it consistently elevated in order for it to heal. I'd gone through these instructions with many Americans who had stubborn leg wounds; their subsequent healing did not involve any brilliance on my part, just a little medical know-how.

Then Michael said, "I have prayed for many years for you to come." His wife said, "We have never lost faith."

We prayed together. Love radiated off Michael and his wife. A feeling of absolute warmth came over me. Sarah had not led me up this hill and into this home; the Christ that we carry around in our hearts had brought us here. On the way out the door, I glanced up at the mud wall. The wisdom from my forgetful patient in residency came back to me. There, written in chalk, was "God Is Love."

There is much work to be done if we are to hand our great-grandchildren a world as good as the one we got. It will take many changes and even sacrifices. Now that the church is taking up the biblical mandate for creation care, I have great optimism. I pray that we will all keep in mind what is important, and that we will carve "God is love" on the tablet of our hearts. We are commissioned to do *God's* will on earth through loving acts of faith. With God, all things are possible.

SERVING GOD, SAVING THE PLANET

A Christian Guide to Action

Chapter 1

1. The author describes the lifestyle changes his family made in response to their conviction to take better care of the earth. What emotions are evoked in you when you imagine yourself making such a choice? Why do you feel that way?

2. The author states that he gained a richer life by giving up material wealth. What do you suppose his losses were? What do you suppose his gains were?

3. "Getting from point A to point B is not always easy, even if you know where A and B are located." What are some of the things that prevent us from making lifestyle changes we know we ought to make? Describe the obstacles in your way. What can help us around them?

4. In what ways is materialism like a tyrant? How have you personally experienced this bondage? How does God as master compare to consumerism as master?

5. The author states that America is addicted to oil. What are some of the signs of an addiction? Do you see any of these signs in American culture? Do you have any signs of addiction to materialism? Explain.

6. The author compares today's dependence on foreign oil to yesteryear's slavery. What similarities do you see? What can we learn from this past mistake in relationship to creation care today?

Chapter 2

1. Dying canaries warned coal miners of problems with the air. What warnings do we have that creation is suffering?

2. "Each new chemical and every pound of exhaust added to the atmosphere is an experiment in just how much we, and the planet, can withstand." Name some toxins we could avoid in our daily lives.

3. When people feel as though the world's problems are too big for them to tackle, they often overlook the decisions they can make to build a better world. What can you do to regain a sense of control and significance? Name three actions you could take this week that would make you part of the cure rather than the problem.

4. When you see others contributing to the environmental problem rather than exercising stewardship, how do you keep from getting angry or discouraged? What advice does Jesus give us about the speck in our neighbor's eye and the log in our own?

5. The key to stop being overwhelmed by the amount of work to be done is to simply take the first step. What will be your first step?

Chapter 3

1. Do you believe churches should be involved in creation care issues? Explain.

2. God gave humans dominion over the earth. The author provides the Hebrew meaning of the word *dominion*: "higher on the root of a plant." How does that definition help you to understand how to treat that which is under human domain?

3. Many people justify their wealth and way of life under the "security" umbrella. What does God teach us about the worldly hunger for permanence and security at any cost? How can material things keep us from a right relationship with God?

4. What examples of environmental changes have you witnessed in your lifetime?

5. List at least three inventions from science that have done more harm than good.

6. "Ten percent of the women and three percent of the men in our country need an antidepressant to get through the day, a day with no fear of starvation, invasion, or want." What factors create this astounding circumstance?

Chapter 4

1. Since you were born, do you think the natural resources in society's "account" have increased or decreased? How has your generation's use of air, land, and water affected future generations?

2. Why do people of faith have a special responsibility toward future generations? What is the relationship between environmental concerns and issues of poverty, health, and compassion?

3. Do you agree that depression may be a warning sign that "we are living a lifestyle God does not sanction or want us to lead?" Explain.

4. The Lord promises to heal our broken hearts. How does nature restore our souls? Explain.

5. When is the last time you glorified God in a place where nothing made by people was in sight? Describe that experience. If you haven't done this in awhile, where could you go in the next week to rest in nature?

Chapter 5

1. According to the parable of the Good Samaritan, who is our neighbor? Going beyond your location and generation, name some people who are in need of neighborly care.

2. Things like televisions and SUVs were not in existence during Jesus's time, so of course the Bible does not mention them. How can we determine the morality of using such items when the Bible doesn't directly address the issue?

3. What is the effect of what the author calls "Orwellian language"? What would happen if people—from politicians to parents to preachers—were more direct in naming their actions? Explain.

4. The author points out that "people who cannot call to mind their last mistake are more likely to make another." What are some useful ways to evaluate our mistakes?

5. What things do you usually thank God for? What are some things you have forgotten to thank God for? Take time now to ask the Holy Spirit to remove any sense of entitlement you might have for material blessings, and be humble in prayer before God.

Chapter 6

1. Do you consider yourself rich? Why or why not?

2. Name at least five things possessions may represent.

3. Do you ever feel that your possessions own you? Explain your answer. What are some other negative effects of wealth?

4. Can you think of any possessions in your house that could be put to better use by someone of lesser means? What are at least three ways you can "lighten up"?

5. The author says that if you are humble about your success, people will ask you for advice, but if you are smug, you will witness to no one. As you grow more successful in your journey away from materialism, how can you best influence others to follow suit?

6. How can becoming a good steward of creation also save you money?

Chapter 7

1. How does the author define work? Name at least three negative effects of not having work in our lives.

2. How can you incorporate work into your daily life?

3. What benefits might you reap if you observed the Sabbath? What benefits might the earth reap if we kept the Sabbath?

4. What factors are keeping you from observing the Sabbath? Name one thing you can do this Sunday to help you keep the Sabbath.

5. What traditions would you like to add to your Sabbath day observations?

Chapter 8

1. What "benefit" do you receive from watching television? What do you lose?

2. How much time per week do you spend watching television? Playing video games? Chatting online? Surfing the Internet?

3. What do television programs and commercials promise? What do they deliver?

4. Compare the amount of time you spend watching TV with the amount of time you spend on other activities. How would you and others benefit from your decision to cut back on television watching?

5. Name three activities that you could do instead of watching television that might bring you closer to God, or help you to better love your neighbor.

Chapter 9

1. How is divorce bad for the environment?

2. How can spoiled or "high maintenance" children hurt a marriage, and the earth?

3. What spiritual lessons do we teach our children when we ask them to recycle paper, take out the compost, and turn out the lights without reminders?

4. What factors in the American fixation on team sports might keep us from God?

5. As the author points out, "We cannot keep our children from the future." How can we best equip our children to face a future that looks uncertain and filled with problems?

Chapter 10

1. What four moral considerations should Christians consider when deciding what to eat?

2. Recall some experiences of eating with others and sharing the same food. What was good about that experience?

3. How do our food choices affect the least among us? How can eating a hamburger at a fast food restaurant in the United States affect a child growing up in sub-Saharan Africa?

4. What is the one commandment of consumerism? How does that affect the way the environment, specifically animals, are treated?

5. What are the benefits of gardening?

Chapter 11

1. If no one can earn their way to heaven, why do we do good deeds?

2. If you did an inventory of the items in your home, would you find yourself lacking or having more than enough? What factors hold you back from giving up some of your possessions?

3. Many people feel better about giving up things when they go directly to people in need. Can you think of area organizations, missions within your church, or specific people that could benefit from things in your home?

4. What can you do to cut down dramatically on the amount of junk mail you receive? Name five other things you could do to reduce your trash production.

5. The author's dramatic lifestyle change "was not an overnight process but an ongoing and continually evolving one." Do you tend to think in an all or nothing mindset, or are you ready to take baby steps toward creation care? What can you do to remain committed to this cause?

Chapter 12

1. How have Jesus and Santa Claus been confused in our modern culture? How has this confusion affected the way we celebrate Christmas?

2. When did you find out Santa Claus was not real? How might this lie affect children?

3. Name at least five ways you could simplify your Christmas season.

4. Name three people in your life who would treasure a letter of thanks more than a material present. What keeps you from giving these people a letter rather than a present?

5. What is the best way you could honor the gift of Christ's birth?

Chapter 13

1. Does it surprise you to learn that the vast majority of your electricity is supplied by coal? Why do you think that only one percent of our electricity comes from clean sources such as solar, wind, geothermal, and biomass combined?

2. Name at least three ways you could immediately start saving electricity.

3. What is the best way for our country to avoid a power shortage in the future? Why do Americans seem to think we will never run out of power?

4. Are Americans preoccupied with power? Explain. How does real or perceived wealth give a person a sense of power?

5. Why do we not feel embarrassed about blatantly polluting the world or expending money frivolously or using up nonrenewable resources? Why does lack of guilt not absolve us of sin?

Chapter 14

1. Have you known anyone who has clung to life too dearly and thereby suffered a miserable and prolonged death? Explain.

2. Why do you think Americans are willing to spend such huge sums of money to gain just a few more months of life? What does the Bible say about these issues?

3. How do you want to spend your last days on earth? Would you want your family to "pull the plug" if your prognosis was terminal and you were unable to communicate your wishes?

4. How do your beliefs about death affect your life?

5. How do you find the balance between caring for your body and obsessing about your health?

Chapter 15

1. Why do we often resist facing stern and unpleasant facts? What does the very nature of the Bible reveal about facing the truth?

2. What myths about overpopulation have you believed?

3. God commanded that we procreate and multiply. How do some people misinterpret that command?

4. Why should Christians be concerned about overpopulation? Who is most affected by this issue?

5. How have humans changed the mortality rates of birth and childhood? How do we forestall death? How does this interference with "natural law" affect the population of Earth?

SERVING GOD, SAVING THE PLANET

Chapter 16

1. What is the most important truth? How can you remember it, even if your memory fails on all other issues?

2. Why does a change of heart often supersede a change of action? How are the two related?

3. Have you ever had the experience of God speaking directly to your heart? Explain. How do you recognize the call of God?

4. When is the last time you asked the crucial question: "Will this bring me closer to God?" What was the result?

5. Now that the church is taking up the biblical mandate for creation care, the author feels very optimistic. How will you become the hands and feet of God, both personally and as a group, in caring for his creation? What could keep you from these commitments? How will you overcome obstacles and continue to grow as responsible stewards?

SERVING GOD, SAVING THE PLANET

APPENDICES

Appendix A

Serving God, Saving the Planet Energy Audit

When I was in undergraduate school, I worked nights and weekends at a hospital—not so that I could put it on my med school application or out of a sense of charity but because Nancy and I were newlyweds and needed the money. My job wasn't in the lab or the X-ray department. No, I was employed as one of the hospital's rent-a-cops. I was hired to keep the drunks in line at night, to take dead bodies to the morgue, and to help out wherever needed.

I was never in too much danger until the time Dr. Beck called two of us for help. On that day I came close to losing my life. One of Dr. Beck's patients had decided to go on a diet. The nurses had tried to weigh her in the office using two scales, but it didn't work, so Dr. Beck decided to try the large platform scale at the hospital's loading dock. The other rent-a-cop and I were asked to escort Mrs. Weed safely to the scale and record her weight. She was gracious and thanked us many times as we traveled down an elevator and back corridor, but her bulk made movement difficult.

As we helped her onto the scale, she began slipping—right on top of me. My colleague yelled, and two men who were on the dock jumped to Mrs. Weed's (and my) rescue. The four of us managed to push her back the few degrees she'd tilted and steady her. We recorded her weight at 636 pounds.

I wondered at the time why Dr. Beck had gone through so

much trouble to have Mrs. Weed weighed. He was a kind and considerate man, and he certainly hadn't wanted to embarrass her or endanger us. When I saw him a week later, he said, "We decided to weigh her because she's gotten serious about losing weight, and I wanted to do what I could to help." Dr. Beck taught me one of life's lessons: We are a society driven by facts and figures. We need a beginning and end point, whether we are losing weight, planning a budget, or going to school. The same is true when we heed the call for planetary stewardship.

What is our environmental "weight"? If we assign weights to the amount of energy used, the average person in China weighs 100 pounds, while the average American weighs an astounding 1,000 pounds. China is too skinny to begin with, you counter? Okay, let's take a country with a considerably higher standard of living than ours. The land of watches, chocolates, and bank accounts is Switzerland. If we put Swiss citizens on the planetary scale, they weigh 450 pounds. On the same scale, Italians weigh about 400 pounds, and the British 500. Even though our British neighbors are large, they can still get around. At 1,000 each, Americans are energy gluttons. We are morbidly obese.

What follows is a simple form to determine just what you or your family's environmental "weight" is. You'll need to gather together a few records, such as annual electricity use, heating oil purchased, and the average miles per gallon reported for each of your cars. If you are not sure how much heating oil you use, call your dealer. Dealers of home heating fuels keep track of each customer's annual usage, as do electricity providers. For annual miles flown, miles driven, and money spent, fill in your best estimate. It's better to go ahead and complete the audit using approximations than not to complete it at all. Dollars spent are converted to their average environmental impact, and everything is then totaled in equivalents of gasoline.

This audit is not designed to become a new form of legalism. We have enough of that in the world. Rather, it is designed to show you how many thousands of gallons of gasoline equivalents it takes to get you and your family through a year of living. My hope is that it also will allow you and your family to live a more equitable and conscientious life. The title of this book is *Serving God, Saving the Planet*. God comes first. If you're using thousands of gallons of fuel a year feeding poor people, running a prisoner visitation program, and distributing Bibles, carry on. You are being a wise steward of your resources. However, most people require a course correction.

In this energy audit, each form of energy—such as electricity or propane—is multiplied by a factor that converts it into the equivalent number of gallons of gasoline. In the following sample audit, I've recorded the energy values for a typical U.S. household. The average U.S. household uses 4,483 gallons of gas (or its equivalent) a year. (The typical single American living alone uses 1,745 gallons.) The average household in China uses about 400 gallons; Italian households use about 1,800 gallons, and the British use about 2,200 gallons per household. Please remember that these are not actual gallons of fuel but "gallon equivalents," which take into account the environmental impact of all our activities and provide a standard energy unit for purposes of comparison.

Most households will not need to fill in every line of the energy audit. For example, most homes do not use city gas and propane and home heating oil. One surprise might be the impact of air travel. Because air travel is so easy and so rapid, it is easy to overlook the impact of a cross-country flight, and yet a round trip from New York to San Diego and back is six thousand miles. If five people in your family travel together on this cross-country trip, that's thirty thousand miles. If you fly for business, you don't need to count those trips—but if you bring your family along, you should count their miles. And if all your business flying earns you free tickets that result in a pleasure trip, that flight counts. Overall, use reason. Count what you can control.

In my story, I forgot to say what got Mrs. Weed off balance. When she stepped up onto the scale, she slipped off her shoes. One would think that a person weighing over six hundred pounds would not worry about the incidental weight of her shoes. When you take your audit, slip off your "shoes" if you feel you must —but remember that underestimating is only cheating yourself.

The reality is that we are such an energy-rich country that our numbers in all the categories are quite large. If this were an audit of Ethiopians, for example, the numbers would be only a fraction of the United States' numbers and therefore more accurate. Nonetheless, the energy audit is an enormously valuable tool for assessing where we stand.

Rome wasn't built in a day, and Mrs. Weed wasn't going to lose five hundred pounds in six months. Similarly, a family that uses five thousand gallons of gasoline equivalents annually is not suddenly going to weigh in like an Italian the following year. It is probably more realistic to set a goal of 10 percent improvement annually.

If you are like me, you will go through a process similar to St. Peter. You will "get it" and work by fits and starts until finally your commitment is firm. Each year will find you saying, "We have too much; how can we use less and give away more?" Always the primary question is: "Does this bring me closer to God?"

The moment you fill out the energy audit, you're serious. If you use less in the future, you will know it. You have a benchmark that, once established, will allow you to make changes and move in the right direction.

Great strides can be made by changing houses or work locations. Exchanging a vehicle that gets 20 miles per gallon for a car that gets 50 miles per gallon can be a painless change. The goal in living a more modest lifestyle is to do less harm, to have more to give away, and to focus on loving others.

Serving God, Saving the Planet Energy Audit

Use your most recent electricity and fuel bills to estimate the following:

Annual kWh of electricity _____ x .06 _____

Annual therms or ccf of natural gas _____ x .88 _____

Annual gallons of #2 fuel oil _____ x 1.23 _____

Annual gallons of propane _____ x .80 **or**

Annual pounds of propane _____ x .19 _____

Annual cords of wood _____ x 220 _____

Car 1:

_____ divided by _____ x 1 _____
miles driven annually   mpg

Car 2:

_____ divided by _____ x 1 _____
miles driven annually   mpg

Car 3:

_____ divided by _____ x 1 _____
miles driven annually   mpg

Diesel vehicle:

_____ divided by _____ x 1.23 _____
miles driven annually   mpg

Miles of airline travel _____ x .044 _____

Gallons of gasoline used annually
(for boats, mowers, snowmobiles,
chainsaws, ATVs, etc.) _____ x 1 _____

Miles of bus travel _____ x .018 _____

Miles of train travel _____ x .013 _____

Total dollars spent annually
(for goods, services, mortgage and
car payments, tuition, travel, etc., but
not including contributions to charity) _____ x .03 _____

TOTAL GALLONS (in gasoline equivalents) _____

Goal for next year _____

How to get there:

Serving God, Saving the Planet Energy Audit
SAMPLE AUDIT (TYPICAL FAMILY), USA

Use your most recent electricity and fuel bills to estimate the following:

Annual kWh of electricity	**12,340**	x .06	**740**
Annual therms or ccf of natural gas		x .88	
Annual gallons of #2 fuel oil	**800**	x 1.23	**984**
Annual gallons of propane	**120**	x .80 **or**	
Annual pounds of propane		x .19	**96**
Annual cords of wood		x 220	

Car 1:

18,120	divided by	**24**	x 1	**755**
miles driven annually		mpg		

Car 2:

10,000	divided by	**30**	x 1	**333**
miles driven annually		mpg		

Car 3:

	divided by		x 1	
miles driven annually		mpg		

Diesel vehicle:

	divided by		x 1.23	
miles driven annually		mpg		

Miles of airline travel	**6,900**	x .044	**304**
Gallons of gasoline used annually (for boats, mowers, snowmobiles, chainsaws, ATVs, etc.)	**50**	x 1	**50**
Miles of bus travel		x .018	
Miles of train travel		x .013	
Total dollars spent annually (for goods, services, mortgage and car payments, tuition, travel, etc., but not including contributions to charity)	**48,500**	x .03	**1,455**

TOTAL GALLONS (in gasoline equivalents)	**4,717**
Goal for next year	**4,245**

How to get there: • *Change lightbulbs* • *Vacation close to home next year* • *Carpool to work* • *Hang laundry on a clothesline in the summer*

The energy audit may suggest new sources of money to give away or to live on. It can be an eye-opener. I'll give you an example. Not long ago, a pastor friend asked me to look at his home and advise him on what he could do to cut his energy bill. His request was motivated not by stewardship so much as by a tight budget. His family has one more person living at home than us. We found that they use just about the same amount of electricity in two months as our home uses annually. The difference represented $2,500—or 10 percent of his take-home pay.

In many countries, one must first "feed the meter"; in other words, change or tokens need to be deposited in the electric meter in order to obtain current. Although we have a different setup, the exchange is just the same. Every time we throw on a light switch, money begins flowing out of our pockets in the opposite direction.

Learn to cut back now. Energy will only keep getting more expensive; the more you save, the greater the rewards you will reap.

Appendix B

Stewardship,
One Appliance at a Time

B elow is a nuts-and-bolts discussion on a question I am frequently asked: How did my family get its average monthly
electrical bill down to $20? I'll answer that question appliance by
appliance, starting with some of the biggest energy users.

Refrigerators

It is a paradox: As the American family eats fewer meals together at
home, the size of the average refrigerator has grown. Many homes
have industrial-size units big enough to service a hospital's kitchen.
Fortunately, selecting a refrigerator that uses the least energy has
become more convenient than ever. The yellow EnergyGuide tags
make "apple to apple" comparisons easy. As with cars, the more
options a refrigerator has, the more electricity it will consume.
One way to make a refrigerator more efficient is to unplug the
automatic ice-maker component. The auto ice-maker uses additional energy in two ways. The obvious one is the motor that can
be heard moving (and in some cases grinding) ice from the storage
bin through a door. The less obvious user of energy is the heating
element that must stay on at all times under the ice-cube-forming
tray. This allows the ice to slide out of the ice-making area into
a storage bin. The effect of the heating element is similar to leaving a lightbulb on inside the freezer. To "upgrade" your current

refrigerator to a more efficient one, disconnect the electrical supply plug to the ice-maker unit and use old-fashioned ice cube trays.

At some point, you may wonder whether it is prudent to get rid of an old refrigerator and purchase a new, more efficient one. There is no hard and fast rule for this. However, I do recommend that you focus on saving electricity before thinking about making electricity through photovoltaic panels or windmills. Using a rule of ten years' or less energy payback as the threshold of replacement, I'll illustrate how you can make a decision to keep or buy new:

The average refrigerator in the United States uses 1,155 kilowatt-hours a year. We bought a refrigerator for our home three years ago. It is 20.6 cubic feet and was rated at 458 kilowatt-hours of consumption a year, before I removed the standard ice-making unit. The electrical rate in our area is 10.7 cents a kilowatt-hour, which means that replacing an average refrigerator with an efficient refrigerator saves (1,155 kWh − 458 kWh) x (10.7 cents kWh) = $74.58 per year, or about $750 in ten years. Since this is more than the cost of our refrigerator, it was probably worth getting a more efficient one. The worst thing you can do, however, is to purchase a new refrigerator *and* keep the old one as well.

Lighting

The second biggest user of electricity in the typical home is lighting. The payoff time for replacing an incandescent bulb averages only about one year; if you buy compact fluorescent lightbulbs on sale or with a rebate, the payback is extremely short. Compact fluorescent bulbs have the added bonus of being safer because they are cooler, which presents far less fire hazard. The typical incandescent wastes 90 percent of the energy it uses by converting it to heat instead of light. In the summer, cooler-running bulbs can have a significant effect on the overall cooling costs of a home or business.

Our entire family has developed the habit of turning off lights when we are going to be out of a room for more than sixty seconds. If you have fixtures in which compact fluorescents are impractical, replace incandescents with lower-wattage halogen bulbs. In some situations, lower-watt halogen bulbs used on dimmers can be almost as efficient as compact fluorescents. LED bulbs use even less energy than compact fluorescents—we use them in places where we leave the light on for long periods of time, like over the kitchen table. For the holidays, consider giving five compact fluorescent bulbs to a friend with a note about Jesus being the light of the world. Include the U.S. government's data (www.energystar.gov) on how changing just five lightbulbs in every household could result in the immediate shutdown of twenty-one coal plants and save thousands of lives.

Television

I don't have subtle views on televisions: I don't like them. I think they have no place in a young child's life and a limited place in older folks' lives. They also happen to be the third largest user of electricity in homes nationwide. Even when not in use, they draw a current. In order for a television to turn on when a remote is used, it must remain partially on at all times. The only way around this is to unplug the TV when it is not in use or to have it on a switched outlet or switched extension cord.

Of all types of televisions, smaller LCD models are the most energy efficient; black-and-white tubes are next. New plasma screens can take 400 watts or more to run. When combined with surround-sound systems, a large-screen TV can use more power

SERVING GOD, SAVING THE PLANET

than refrigeration. The practice of having multiple televisions on in a house is particularly wasteful.

Unplug TVs when they're not in use. Turn them off when you're not in the room. Watch for fewer hours, and never fall asleep with one on. Falling asleep with a television on is like leaving your car running for the night.

Audio Equipment

I place music — and the ability to reproduce it at any time — on the "top five" list of modern inventions I'd least want to give up. Adding beauty to life, however, must be balanced with the obsession for the new and novel. Do you really need the latest format? Do mp3s sound better than HDCD? Are CDs better than compact cassettes or eight tracks? What was wrong with the way music made you feel when it was played on the record player?

The U.S. government reports that Americans spend more money to power audio equipment when it is off than when it is on. When stereos are off—which is most of the time—they are still using energy because they are in standby mode. Make sure to get power strips for audio equipment so that it can be turned completely off. If you don't know whether your audio equipment has a "phantom load" or draws current when it is off, here are two clues: If it has a remote control that can turn it on, or if it has an instant-on feature, then it constantly draws and uses electricity even when in the off mode. If it has a clock or LED lights, it is always on.

Dryers

Electric clothes dryers use energy at a rate of 5,000 watts. That's 5 kilowatt-hours for the average one-hour load. Units that sense humidity in the clothes and cut off when items are dry rather than running timed cycles are more efficient. Cleaning lint and venting dryers with metal hosing will increase the efficiency and safety of dryers.

As I've said earlier, my family has chosen not to own a dryer. Our clothes last longer when dried outside and smell of fresh air. I use this time for prayer.

In the winter, we dry our clothing indoors on a retractable line that runs along the south-facing windows. We also have a bar that hangs in front of our wood stove. Both of these methods not only dry the clothing safely without electricity but also add humidity to our winter indoor air, which helps maintain a healthy home.

Microwaves

Although microwaves draw a large current, they do so for a short period of time. Overall, microwaving is one of the most efficient ways to cook. Buy the smallest unit that you can and get one with analog controls (no key pad or clock) so that it is not constantly drawing current. Whenever possible, use your microwave to pre-cook food so that you can cut back on the use of bigger appliances, such as your oven.

Computers

Computer ownership and usage continues to grow rapidly. Energy Star units that place computers in sleep mode when unattended are preferable to non-Energy Star models; however, try to get out of the habit of leaving a computer (or any appliance) on and unattended. In general, laptop models will draw about half the current of desktop models. All desktop models should be plugged into an outlet strip so that the phantom load can be completely turned off. Be sure to turn off printers when they are not in use.

Stoves

There are three major types of cookstoves: those that run on electricity, on natural gas, and on propane. One question that might come up is "Should I switch from my electric stove to a gas stove?" The answer is yes and no. If there is nothing wrong with your electric unit, the answer is probably no. If your stove is broken or you are building a new home, go with gas or propane. In general, switching to a gas stove that has no pilot light is preferable — provided you don't buy a huge stainless-steel industrial-size model. In order to make a watt of electrical energy that will be used at home, three watts must initially be produced at the power plant. This is because two-thirds of the energy goes up smokestacks and cooling towers, and because energy is lost in the long-distance transmission process. Any path greater than one hundred feet is a long distance in the physics of electrical transmission.

Buy the smallest possible appliance or unit that will work for your family. Use a toaster oven when possible. Our family bakes a loaf of bread every few days. We've found the bread-making machine to be more energy efficient than baking in an oven. When we bought a stove, we found one that has no phantom electric loads and has a smaller-than-usual oven.

Some Luxury Items

Hot Tubs

To operate a hot tub in my area of the country and run it off solar power would take an investment of $50,000 in solar panels and inverters (give or take $10,000 — most likely give). If the average hot tub is used half an hour a day, that means it remains unoccupied 98 percent of the time.

It would seem that communities, not individuals, should own

and operate hot tubs. The typical spa uses 2,300 kilowatt-hours per year in energy. It is difficult to imagine that we will get to heaven and share all things if we don't get a little practice here on earth. Hot tubs, pools, lawn tractors, and pickup trucks are just a few of the items that future saints should figure out how to share.

Pools

Pool pumps and filters are big users of electricity. I once heard a sales clerk in a hardware store complain that her electricity bill went up $200 per month during the time she opened her swimming pool. One way to lessen the energy load of a pool is to use ionization technology that works on solar power.

However, take note that some products sold "to help the planet" may not help but actually harm. There is a trend to market products under the heading of "eco" or "solar." Often these products are not necessary and simply detract from a family's mission to use less, reduce, and reuse.

Below is an incomplete list of electrical devices you may want but probably don't *need*:

- Aquariums
- Lava lamps
- Air purifiers
- Blenders
- Electric carving knives
- Electric toothbrushes and toothbrush sanitizers
- Leaf blowers
- Coffee warmers
- Electric doorbells
- Fountains
- Multiple clocks
- Hot curlers, curling irons, and hair straighteners
- Electric air fresheners
- Electric treadmills, stationary bikes, and other exercise equipment
- Electric staplers
- Electric games

Let It Begin with Me: An Earth Care To-Do List

*Even so faith, if it hath not works, is dead, being
alone. Yea, a man may say, Thou hast faith, and I
have works: shew me thy faith without thy works,
and I will shew thee my faith by my works.*

— James 2:17 – 18 KJV

To preserve and restore God's creation, you will need to put faith into action. Below are some practical actions you can take — today, this week, this month, and this year — to begin your ecological walk with God the Creator. The precursor to action is prayer. You must prayerfully begin by humbling yourself before God and acknowledging a desire to change. In submitting to his will, you will gain the strength necessary to break old habits and form new ones.

If this prayer list looks daunting at first, then just start with one change. And remember, the most important change you can make is in your heart. Everything else will follow.

*Dear Heavenly Father: Thank you for the bounty of your gifts,
for the beauty of your created world, and for the sustenance you
provide me every day, both physical and spiritual. Thank you
for giving me everything I need in such glorious abundance —
from the air I breathe to the water I drink to the food I put upon
the table. Please forgive me for taking your creation for granted,
and give me the strength and will to become a better steward of*

your blessings. Teach me to appreciate all you have given me, and help me to restore the forests, mountains, rivers, and oceans so that they can glorify you, the creator of heaven and earth.

Lord, help me TODAY to:
- ○ Memorize a Bible verse about God's love for his creation (see Appendix E for suggestions).
- ○ Pray for people whose forests and habitats have been destroyed by my material desires.
- ○ Pick up and throw away any trash I see on the ground.
- ○ Turn off the faucet while brushing my teeth and shaving.
- ○ Turn my thermostat up three degrees (in summer) or down three degrees (in winter).
- ○ Wash my dishes by hand, or if I use the dishwasher, run it only with a full load, and not use heat for the drying cycle.
- ○ Wash my clothes in the coolest water possible.
- ○ Turn off the lights, TV, radio, and stereo when I leave the room for more than sixty seconds.
- ○ Give something away.
- ○ Spend at least ten minutes with you—quietly—in nature.
- ○ Use the money I save to advance your kingdom.

What doth it profit, my brethren, though a man say he hath faith, and have not works? Can faith save him? (James 2:14 KJV)

Lord, help me THIS WEEK to:
- ○ Read Psalms 23, 24, 104, 147, and 148.
- ○ Take a day of rest—no shopping, no work, no driving.
- ○ Bike, walk, carpool, or use public transportation instead of driving.

- ○ Avoid the mall completely.
- ○ Visit the grocery store only once.
- ○ Consciously combine trips and errands.
- ○ Recycle everything I can.
- ○ Change at least five lightbulbs in my home to compact fluorescents.
- ○ Buy only fair-trade and shade-grown coffee and other sustainably grown foods.
- ○ Donate a box of books to the library.
- ○ Buy only "tree free" toilet paper, paper towels, and tissues made from recycled paper.
- ○ Air-dry my laundry.
- ○ Hand-wash clothes instead of taking them to the dry cleaner.
- ○ Precycle by buying minimally packaged goods and choosing reusable over disposable.
- ○ Cut back on the amount of junk mail I receive by registering at www.dmachoice.org or writing to Mail Preference Service, P.O. Box 643, Carmel, NY, 10512. (Include date, name, address, and signature, along with the message "Please register my name with the Mail Preference Service." Enclose a $1 check payable to DMA for processing.
- ○ Avoid fast-food restaurants.
- ○ Eat at least one meatless lunch and dinner this week.
- ○ Check out a faith-based organization working to save God's created earth.

Ye see then how that by works a man is justified, and not by faith only.... For as the body without the spirit is dead, so faith without works is dead also. (James 2:24, 26 KJV)

Lord, help me THIS MONTH to:

- ○ Stock up on handkerchiefs, cloth shopping bags, and cloth napkins so I can kick the paper habit.
- ○ Clean out my closets and donate clothes I have not worn in the past year.
- ○ Start a weekly or monthly family night where we eat dinner together, play games, or read a book aloud.
- ○ Compost my food and yard waste.
- ○ Wait a month before buying something I "need"; when I do make purchases, let me buy quality items that will last for many years.
- ○ Install low-flow showerheads.
- ○ Replace church lightbulbs with compact fluorescents.
- ○ Talk to my church and workplace about using recycled paper in copying machines and printers.
- ○ Buy produce locally and support organic family farms.
- ○ Clean or replace air filters throughout my house.
- ○ Wrap my hot water heater in an insulating jacket if it is over five years old and has no internal insulation.
- ○ Caulk and weather-strip around my windows and doors to plug air leaks.
- ○ Save all the catalogs that I don't want to receive and call each one, asking to be taken off its mailing list.
- ○ Disconnect the ice maker in my freezer.
- ○ Unplug the TV and stereo when not in use, or put them on a switched power strip or outlet.

○ Volunteer to help people who have fewer resources than I do.

> But be ye doers of the word, and not hearers only, deceiving your own selves. For if any be a hearer of the word, and not a doer, he is like unto a man beholding his natural face in a glass. For he beholdeth himself, and goeth his way, and straightway forgetteth what manner of man he was. But whoso looketh into the perfect law of liberty, and continueth therein, he being no a forgetful hearer, but a doer of the work, this man shall be blessed in his deed. (James 1:22–25 KJV)

Lord, help me **THIS YEAR** to:

○ Organize a prayer group, volunteer for a short-term mission, or ask my church to adopt a village, with a focus on honoring our Creator by honoring his creation.

○ Plant deciduous trees along the south side of my house to save on cooling costs.

○ Donate my old cell phone, computer, or printer to a good cause.

○ Set up a recycling program at my workplace, church, or school.

○ Cut way back on the Christmas frenzy.

○ Set up a share board in my church or organize a clothing exchange.

○ Start a tool library or toy library in my town or church.

○ Give away or sell anything and everything that is cluttering my life. Donate the proceeds to charity.

○ Use no pesticides or chemicals on my lawn or garden.

○ Instead of a birthday gift or flowers for a funeral, send a donation to charity.

○ Pick one endangered species and do something to help save it.

○ When appliances and lighting fixtures need to be replaced, purchase only the most efficient Energy Star items.

○ Start a vegetable garden at home, or organize a community or church garden and donate some of the harvest to local homeless shelters and soup kitchens.

○ Stay closer to home on my next family trip and stay home on one holiday when I usually travel.

○ Organize a church-based public prayer event with emphasis on creation care and stewardship.

○ Ask my church to adopt a local stream, park, or roadway for cleanup, monitoring, and restoration.

○ Start a study group on what the Bible says about caring for creation.

○ Ask my utility company to conduct an energy audit on my home and follow up on their advice, and do the same for my church.

○ Insulate my walls and ceilings to save up to 25 percent on my energy bill.

○ If I need to replace my windows, install the most efficient, energy-saving models.

○ When I replace my car, purchase a hybrid or one that gets great mileage and has low emissions.

○ Organize a paint swap at my church or recycling center; combine unused portions of paint and use as primer.

○ Follow our grandmothers' advice: "Use it up, wear it out, make it do, or do without."

Visit www.blessedearth.org to learn more about what the Bible says concerning earth care and to find more practical ways to conserve resources.

Appendix D

Environmental Scripture References

In the beginning God created the heavens and the earth.... God saw all that he had made, and it was very good.

—Genesis 1:1, 31

I now establish my covenant with you and with your descendants after you and with every living creature that was with you—the birds, the livestock and all the wild animals, all those that came out of the ark with you—every living creature on earth.

—Genesis 9:9–10

The land itself must observe a sabbath to the LORD. For six years sow your fields, and for six years prune your vineyards and garner their crops. But in the seventh year the land is to have a year of sabbath rest, a sabbath to the LORD.... The land is to have a year of rest.

—Leviticus 25:2–5

Follow my decrees and be careful to obey my laws, and you will live safely in the land. Then the land will yield its fruit, and you will eat your fill and live there in safety....

The land must not be sold permanently, because the

land is mine and you reside in my land as foreigners and
strangers.

—Leviticus 25:18–19, 23

To the LORD your God belong the heavens, even the
highest heavens, the earth and everything in it.

—Deuteronomy 10:14

Yours, LORD, is the greatness and the power
  and the glory and the majesty and the splendor,
  for everything in heaven and earth is yours.

—1 Chronicles 29:11

You alone are the LORD. You made the heavens, even
the highest heavens, and all their starry host, the earth
and all that is on it, the seas and all that is in them. You
give life to everything, and the multitudes of heaven
worship you.

—Nehemiah 9:6

Ask the animals, and they will teach you,
  or the birds in the sky, and they will tell you;
or speak to the earth, and it will teach you,
  or let the fish of the sea inform you.
Which of all these does not know
  that the hand of the Lord has done this?
In his hand is the life of every creature
  and the breath of all mankind.

—Job 12:7–10

He spreads out the northern skies over empty space;
  he suspends the earth over nothing.
He wraps up the waters in his clouds,
  yet the clouds do not burst under their weight.

He covers the face of the full moon,
    spreading his clouds over it....
The pillars of the heavens quake,
    aghast at his rebuke.
By his power he churned up the sea....
By his breath the skies become fair....
And these are but the outer fringe of his works;
    how faint the whisper we hear of him!
How then can we understand the thunder
      of his power?

                      —Job 26:7−9, 11−14

The heavens declare the glory of God;
    the skies proclaim the work of his hands.
Day after day they pour forth speech;
    night after night they reveal knowledge.
They have no speech, they use no words;
    no sound is heard from them.
Yet their voice goes out into all the earth,
    their words to the ends of the world.

                      —Psalm 19:1−4

The earth is the LORD's, and everything in it,
    the world, and all who live in it.

                      —Psalm 24:1

For the LORD is the great God,
    the great King above all gods.
In his hand are the depths of the earth,
    and the mountain peaks belong to him.
The sea is his, for he made it,
    and his hands formed the dry land.

                      —Psalm 95:3−5

Sing to the LORD a new song;
  sing to the LORD, all the earth....
Let the heavens rejoice, let the earth be glad;
  let the sea resound, and all that is in it.
Let the fields be jubilant, and everything in them;
  let all the trees of the forest sing for joy.

  —Psalm 96:1, 11–12

How many are your works, LORD!
  In wisdom you made them all;
  the earth is full of your creatures.
There is the sea, vast and spacious,
  teeming with creatures beyond number—
  living things both large and small.

  —Psalm 104:24–25

Praise the LORD from the earth,
  you great sea creatures and all ocean depths,
lightning and hail, snow and clouds,
  stormy winds that do his bidding,
you mountains and all hills,
  fruit trees and all cedars,
wild animals and all cattle,
  small creatures and flying birds.

  —Psalm 148:7–10

The desert and the parched land will be glad;
  the wilderness will rejoice and blossom.
Like the crocus, it will burst into bloom;
  it will rejoice greatly and shout for joy....
Water will gush forth in the wilderness
  and streams in the desert.

  —Isaiah 35:1–2, 6

Who has measured the waters in the hollow of his hand,
    or with the breadth of his hand marked off the heavens?
Who has held the dust of the earth in a basket,
    or weighed the mountains on the scales
    and the hills in a balance?...
Lift up your eyes and look to the heavens:
    Who created all these?
He who brings out the starry host one by one
    and calls forth each of them by name.

—Isaiah 40:12, 26

The wild animals honor me,
    the jackals and the owls,
because I provide water in the wilderness.

—Isaiah 43:20

Hear the word of the LORD, you Israelites,
    because the LORD has a charge to bring
    against you who live in the land:
"There is no faithfulness, no love,
    no acknowledgment of God in the land.
There is only cursing, lying and murder,
    stealing and adultery;
they break all bounds,
    and bloodshed follows bloodshed.
Because of this the land dries up,
    and all who live in it waste away;
the beasts of the field, the birds in the sky
    and the fish in the sea are swept away."

—Hosea 4:1–3

But the worries of this life, the deceitfulness of wealth and the desires for other things come in and choke the word, making it unfruitful.

—Mark 4:19

Then he said to them, "Watch out! Be on your guard against all kinds of greed; life does not consist in an abundance of possessions."

—Luke 12:15

Consider how the wild flowers grow. They do not labor or spin. Yet I tell you, not even Solomon in all his splendor was dressed like one of these.

—Luke 12:27

Through him all things were made; without him nothing was made that has been made.

—John 1:3

For since the creation of the world God's invisible qualities—his eternal power and divine nature—have been clearly seen, being understood from what has been made.

—Romans 1:20

You are worthy, our Lord and God,
    to receive glory and honor and power,
for you created all things,
    and by your will they were created
    and have their being.

—Revelation 4:11

Christians on Creation Care

The initial step for a soul to come to knowledge of God is contemplation of nature.

—Irenaeus

I want creation to penetrate you with so much admiration that wherever you go, the least plant may bring you the clear remembrance of the Creator.... One blade of grass or one speck of dust is enough to occupy your entire mind in beholding the art with which it has been made.

—St. Basil the Great

The world has been created for everyone's use, but you few rich are trying to keep it for yourselves. For not merely the possession of the earth, but the very sky, the air, and the sea are claimed for the use of the rich few.... The earth belongs to all, not just to the rich.

—St. Ambrose of Milan

Some people, in order to discover God, read books. But there is a great book: the very appearance of created things. Look above you! Look below you! Read it. God, whom you want to discover, never wrote that book with ink. Instead He set before your eyes the things that He had made. Can you ask for a louder voice than that?

—St. Augustine

We should remain within the limits imposed by our basic needs and strive with all our power not to exceed them. Once we are carried beyond these limits in our desire for the pleasures of life, there is no criterion to check our onwards movement, since no bounds can be set to that which exceeds the necessary.

—St. Nilus of Ancyra

We shall awaken from our dullness and rise vigorously toward justice. If we fall in love with creation deeper and deeper, we will respond to its endangerment with passion.

—Hildegard of Bingen

Any error about creation also leads to an error about God.

—Thomas Aquinas

If thy heart were right, then every creature would be a mirror of life and a book of holy doctrine. There is no creature so small and abject, but it reflects the goodness of God.

—Thomas à Kempis

God writes the Gospel, not in the Bible alone, but also on trees, and in the flowers and clouds and stars.

—Martin Luther

The creation is quite like a spacious and splendid house, provided and filled with the most exquisite and the most abundant furnishings. Everything in it tells us of God.

—John Calvin

We give you thanks, most gracious God, for the beauty
    of the earth and sky and sea;
for the richness of mountains, plains, and rivers;
for the songs of birds and the loveliness of flowers.
We praise you for these good gifts and pray that we may
    safeguard them for our posterity.
Grant that we may continue to grow in our grateful
    enjoyment of your abundant creation,
to the honor and glory of your name, now and forever.

—The Book of Common Prayer

I believe in my heart that faith in Jesus Christ can and will lead us beyond an exclusive concern for the well-being of other human beings to the broader concern for the well-being of the birds in our backyards, the fish in our rivers, and every living creature on the face of the earth.

—John Wesley

All abuse and waste of God's creatures are spoil and robbery on the property of the Creator.

—Adam Clarke

If it were not for the outside world, we should have no inside world to understand things by. Least of all could we understand God without these millions of sights and sounds and scents and motions weaving their endless harmonies. They come out of His heart to let us know a little of what is in it.

—George MacDonald

I love to think of nature as an unlimited broadcasting station through which God speaks to us every hour, if we will only tune in.

—George Washington Carver

A wrong attitude toward nature implies, somewhere, a wrong attitude toward God.

—T. S. Eliot

A society in which consumption has to be artificially stimulated in order to keep production going is a society founded on trash and waste, and such a society is a house built upon sand.

—Dorothy Sayers

Because God created the natural—invented it out of His love and artistry—it demands our reverence.

—C. S. Lewis

We need to find God, but we cannot find him in noise or in excitement. See how nature, the trees, the flowers, the grass grow in deep silence. See how the stars, the moon, and the sun all move in silence.

—Mother Teresa

To drive to extinction something He has created is wrong. He has a purpose for everything....

We Christians have a responsibility to take the lead in caring for the earth.

—Billy Graham

The seriousness of ecological degradation lays bare the depth of man's moral crisis.... Simplicity, moderation and discipline, as well as the spirit of sacrifice, must become a part of everyday life.

—Pope John Paul II

The best remedy for those who are afraid, lonely or unhappy is to go outside, somewhere where they can be quiet, alone with the heavens, nature and God. Because only then does one feel that all is as it should be and that God wishes to see people happy, amidst the simple beauty of nature.... I firmly believe that nature brings solace in all troubles.

—Anne Frank

We must work passionately and indefatigably to bridge the gulf between our scientific progress and our moral progress. One of the great problems of mankind is that we suffer from a poverty of the spirit which stands in glaring contrast to our scientific and technological abundance. The richer we have become materially, the poorer we have become morally and spiritually.

—Martin Luther King Jr.

Acknowledgments

With a thankful heart and much love, I wish to acknowledge the indispensable help of Alan and Anne Barker, who started this journey with us back in medical school

My dedicated medical colleagues, including Peggy Pinkham, Carolyn Foster, and the staff of St. Andrews Hospital, who set an example of service and compassionate care

Our friends and neighbors in Maine, especially Scott and Joanie Benoit Samuelson, P.J. and Jennifer Kimball, and John and Susan Lord, who took us camping and maple sugaring and shared their love of Casco Bay

Rev. Don and Mary Elise Thomas, who welcomed us to Monroe and passed along a lifetime of godly wisdom

Bev Everett, librarian extraordinaire, for patiently typing the manuscript

Headmaster Tom Lovett and the faculty and staff at St. Johnsbury Academy, who offered our children a world-class education, blessed Nancy with a wonderful teaching position, and opened their campus to our message

George, Barbara, Amanda, and Melinda Cobb for being my ever-faithful fans in the pews

Margie and Steve Hofberg, for making their house our second home

Rev. Jim Ball, Rev. Richard Cizik, and the many other visionaries who paved the way for the creation care message

Florence Heacock, Carol Steele, and Allison Fisher for helping
with congregations in the DC area

Rev. Walt Edmunds, Judge Scott and Cindy Fulton, Jeff and
Cathy Heinbaugh, Pam Colburn, Joyce Dooley, and all our church
friends in Damascus for sponsoring our ministry

Bee Morehead, Brooke Ferguson, Nan Hildreth, Anna Clark,
Nelda Mills, Smitty, and all the great people in the Lone Star state
for their Texas-style hospitality

Prime Time America producer Kelly Pena, Moody Broadcasting host Roy Patterson, author Bill McKibben, Christian writer
Michael Barrick, and all the radio, television hosts, and journalists
who have communicated the urgent need to care for creation

My high school friend Bobby Coddington and Sue Smith, for
donating Bibles

Rosie Schaap and the incredibly kind folks at *Guideposts* for
sponsoring a year-long series on earth stewardship

Margo Baldwin, John Barstow, Alice Blackmer, Beau Fried-
lander, Marcy Brandt, Collette Leonard, Jon-Mikel Gates, Minda
Kaufman, and Jonathan Teller who helped launch this book

Pastor Paul and Betty Powers, our faith group, Dr. Chris and
Sara Plumley, and our brothers and sisters at Union Baptist Church,
for their prayers and spiritual guidance

Lisa Renstrom, for her gracious hospitality

Film producers/directors Michael Taylor, Karen Coshoff, Jeff
Gibbs, Chris Henze, and Jen Kaplan for their vision

Charlie Howell, Jeff Barrie, Alex Tapia, Dave Pelton, and the
people at Trust for the Future, for partnering with us

Ben Lowe, Lindy Scott, and Duane Litfin of Wheaton College; Jerry Cain of Judson College; the chaplains of Middlebury
College; and the many, many colleges and universities who have
opened their campuses

Andy Crouch and John Wilson of *Christianity Today*, for their early support and generous spirits

Peter and Miranda Harris and Ben Campbell of A Rocha, for heralding creation care as a Christian call on the international level

The faculty, staff, and students at Asbury College, for embracing us, especially Josh Lallatin, our multitalented "Chief of Staff," and Dr. Glen Spann, our pastor/in-house historian, and his beautiful wife Shelly

Sandy Vander Zicht, Scott Heagle, and the entire Christ-centered staff of Zondervan, for their expert advice, warm welcome, and ongoing support

The hundreds of congregations that have invited me to speak

The many faith groups, book studies, and Sunday school groups who are using *Serving God, Saving the Planet* for study

The students at Good Shepherd who sang to me

The many, many people who have opened their homes to us while we travel; you are the model of Godly hospitality

Dr. John and Margie Haley, for their generous and on-going sustenance

Very special thanks from the bottom of our hearts to Dr. John and Cindy Spicer; the Lord continues to bless us with your unflagging support, your fellowship, and your love—we could not do this without you

Most of all, my son Clark and daughter Emma, for listening to my stories ... repeatedly, for following Christ's call to be a light unto the world, for hanging laundry and becoming the best-ever energy star dishwashers, and for being two of the people I most love in this world.

May God continue to bless all those who made this book possible and those—far too many to list—who show their love for God by loving His creation.

May all glory be to God!

The Blessed Earth Story

Matthew Sleeth was an ER doctor and chief of staff at a New England hospital when his wife, Nancy, asked him a life changing question: "What's the biggest problem facing the world today?" His reply: "The earth is dying." Nancy's second question was harder to answer, "If the earth is dying, what are we going to do about it?"

Leading by example, Dr. Sleeth left his medical career and moved with his family to a house the size of their old garage, reducing their energy usage by more than two-thirds and cutting back their trash production by nine-tenths. In 2008, the Sleeths started Blessed Earth, an educational nonprofit that inspires and equips people of faith to become better stewards of the earth.

Explore the Blessed Earth website (blessedearth.org) to learn more about creation care books and films, download practical tools, sign up for the monthly e-newsletter, and share inspiring stories.

Serving God, Saving the Planet Guidebook with DVD

A Call to Care for Creation and Your Soul

J. Matthew Sleeth, MD

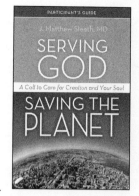

Serving God, Saving the Planet is a video-based learning experience that will broaden the conversation with a focus on the dangers of materialism, workaholism, and spiritual bankruptcy — as well as God's endless invitations for us to enjoy what he has created. This twelve-session video-based study, with participant's guide, provides simple, everyday ways to focus on stewardship and sustainability according to Scripture.

In the first six sessions, Dr. Matthew Sleeth explores his personal salvation experience and desire to follow Jesus in the context of the love story God tells in Genesis. Dr. Sleeth guides us through each of the created elements — Light, Water, Soil, Heavens, Animals, and Man — and reminds us of our God-given commission to "tend and protect the planet." In the final six sessions, Dr. Sleeth examines how God's original command to "tend and protect the planet" extends into the actions and activities of our everyday lives.

This curriculum pack contains one *Serving God, Saving the Planet* DVD and one *Serving God, Saving the Planet Participant's Guide*.

Available in stores and online!